MARIJUANA
Grow Basics

MARIJUANA
Grow Basics

**The Easy Guide for
Cannabis Aficionados**

JORGE CERVANTES

Van Patten Publishing

Cover design: Jorge Cervantes, J. C. Thompson, Alan Dubinsky

Cover photos: Jorge Cervantes, J. C. Thompson

Back cover photo: Jorge Cervantes

Artwork: Chris Valdes

Book design: Susan Applegate, rosa+wesley, inc.

Editors: Linda Meyer, Estella Cervantes

for Contributors, photographers and more credits see page 221 "Acknowledgments."

Photograph on page two: Jorge's Diamonds #1

This book is written for the purpose of supplying information to the public. The publisher, author, and others associated with the production of this book do not advocate breaking the law. All text and illustrations are for descriptive purposes only.

The publisher and the authors do not recommend you try anything presented in this book. You are encouraged to read any and all information available about cannabis to develop a complete background on the subject.

The author and publisher have tried to the best of their abilities to describe the most current cannabis growing methods. However, there may be some mistakes in the text that the author and publisher were unable to detect. This book contains current information up to the date of publication.

Neither the publisher nor the author endorses any products or brand names that are mentioned or pictured in the text. These products are mentioned or pictured for illustration only. Any advice provided in this book—electrical, legal, financial, scientific, etc.— is given for example only. Neither the publisher nor the author assumes any responsibility for any actions associated with this advice.

Published by Van Patten Publishing, Inc. USA. Check **www.vanpattenpublishing.com** for details.

Printed in China

9 8 7 6 5 4 3 2

ISBN-13: 978-1-878823-37-3

*This book is dedicated
to all the growers
in the world!*

Contents

CHAPTER 4
Vegetative Growth

CHAPTER 5
Pre-flowering

CHAPTER 6
Flowering

CHAPTER 7
Clones and
Mother Plants

Introduction

This book is designed to show everyone the basic things you need to know to grow a great crop of marijuana indoors.

Upon finishing *Marijuana Horticulture: The Indoor/Outdoor Grower's Bible*, novice growers from Brazil, Japan, France, Germany, Poland, Portugal, Russia, Spain, the USA, the UK, and several other countries personally asked me for a scaled-down version of the *Bible*. Here it is, *Marijuana Grow Basics: The Easy Guide for Cannabis Aficionados*. This image-based guide with more pictures and less text is designed to give indoor growers enough information to cultivate great crops, but not so much text that they are overwhelmed by horticultural concepts. Reading this book will be like going on a tour of the 150 different grow rooms that I visited to collect information and photos for this book.

Before we look at the plant and what it needs to grow, I'll share some organizational info to help you make the best use of this guidebook.

This Book is Organized into Five Basic Parts

1. **How a plant grows:** this section takes you through the entire process from seed or clone through harvesting, manicuring, and storing the finished product.
2. **Grow gear:** all the things necessary to grow a good crop.
3. **Growing the crop:** this section shows you how to set up your grow room and get growing. You will also learn about pests, diseases, and troubleshooting your crop.
4. **Examples** of 54 specific gardens.
5. **Pests, diseases, and problems**

NOTE: A Sea of Green (SOG) garden is one that consists of short plants that grow closely together and mimic a sea of green. Any garden with plants huddled closely together qualifies as a sea of green. You can find many gardens in this book that qualify as a sea of green even though they may not be labeled as such. A Screen of Green Garden (SCROG) is like a sea of green garden but it has a horizontal trellis (screen) to train fewer bud-laden plants upright.

NOTE: Metric conversions are approximate.

NOTE: Abbreviations: THC (tetrahidrocannabinol), CBD (cannabidiol), CBN (cannabinol).

CHAPTER 1

ABCs of Growing Indoors

INTRODUCTION

The basics necessary to grow indoors are easy. Find a secure location, plant good seeds or clones, create the proper climate—air, light water, nutrients, drainage, and growing medium—and start growing. Seeds soon turn into seedlings, and then put on leafy vegetative growth. They show male or female pre-flowers at the end of the vegetative growth stage. Once flowering is induced, your marijuana plants will be ready to harvest in about two months. Read on and fill your mind with images to learn all the details!

Security
- Never tell anybody about any garden!
- Never show your garden to anyone!
- Read **Chapter 2: Security** twice!

Seeds

Cannabis (aka marijuana or marihuana) seeds like these California Orange are easy to purchase via mail order. You can buy them from seed companies that advertise in the magazines *High Times, Cannabis Culture, Soft Secrets, Weed World, Cañamo, Grow, Dolce Vita*, etc. Or you can find them on the Internet by typing "marijuana seeds" into the www.google.com search engine. Sometimes you will find seeds in buds. To learn more about seeds, see Chapter 3: Seeds and Germination.

Clones

Clones are branch tips cut from female marijuana plants and rooted. Clones are desirable because they are female and will flower sooner than seeds. A crop of clones can be harvested in about three months. Clones are not available by mail order. You must get them from a grower, friend of a grower, or medical marijuana cooperative. Learn more about clones in Chapter 7: Clones and Mother Plants.

A Space to Grow

A grow space is easy to find in any home or structure. The grow space should be enclosed so that you can control the environment inside where the plants will grow. You can close off a corner of the basement, the attic, or a room on the main floor to make a grow room. Use plastic, wood or brick to enclose the room. You can also convert a closet into a grow room, or you can purchase a prefabricated grow cabinet or closet. See Chapter 10: Grow Cabinets, Closets, and Rooms.

Temperature Control

The temperature and humidity in grow space will need to be controlled. The ideal temperature for cannabis growth is about 75°F (24°C). The ideal humidity for cannabis growth is 50–70 percent for pre-flowering and 50 percent for flowering plants. Chances are the environment will need to be heated or cooled a little to maintain the ideal temperature and humidity. Often a ventilation fan (see below) is all you need to keep the temperature and humidity perfect. Learn more about heating and cooling in Chapter 10: Grow Cabinets, Closets, and Rooms.

Air Circulation

Marijuana uses carbon dioxide (CO_2) from the air. The CO_2 is used up quickly around foliage, and the air must be circulated so that new CO_2 comes in contact with leaves. You will need an oscillating circulation fan to keep the air stirred up and CO_2 readily available for plant intake. A circulation fan will also mix the hot air on top and cool air below so the temperature is even throughout the room. See Chapter 10: Grow Cabinets, Closets, and Rooms for details.

Air Ventilation

Marijuana uses all the available CO_2 in a room pretty fast. A ventilation fan expels used CO_2-poor air. The vent fan also removes hot, humid air from the grow space. Fresh, cool, dry air rich in CO_2 is drawn into the room via a fresh-air intake vent. See Chapter 10: Grow Cabinets, Closets, and Rooms for details.

Light

Provide light with fluorescent tubes, compact fluorescent lamps (CFLs), metal halide lamps, or high pressure (HP) sodium lamps. Each lamp has positive points and limiting points. Fluorescent lamps are best suited to growing seedlings and clones. Inexpensive CFLs can grow small crops from start to finish. The best CFLs for growing are available in wattages from 65–125. More expensive and versatile metal halide and HP sodium high intensity discharge (HID) lamps are available in many wattages (from 150–1500) and color spectrums. Both can be used to grow crops from beginning to end. See Chapter 9: Grow Gear for details.

Water and Drainage

Ordinary tap water is usually adequate to grow cannabis. If it is okay to drink, it is usually okay for your plants. If your water tastes bad and is full of sodium and other minerals, you may need to treat it with a reverse osmosis filter. Such control is usually not necessary when growing with soil. See Chapter 9: Grow Gear for details.

Hydroponics

"Hydroponics" means growing in a soilless mix that serves to anchor plant roots. Hydroponics allows the grower to control fertilizer (nutrient) levels and uptake by plants. Hydroponic grow mediums provide more air space around roots, and nutrient uptake is faster than in soil gardens. Hydroponic gardens require more control of water, pH, nutrients, and the root-zone environment. Hydroponic gardens can be very simple and inexpensive or complex and expensive. For more information see Chapter 9: Grow Gear.

Soil

Growing in soil is simple and easy. Always purchase good soil that drains well. If you cannot find good soil, mix your own from quality components. Organic soil gardens boast the best flavor and fragrance. See Chapter 9: Grow Gear for more information on soil mixes.

Cannabis Life Cycle and Indoor Growing

Introduction

Cannabis cultivated indoors needs light (1), air (2), a growing medium (3), warmth (4), nutrients (5), and water (6). As explained earlier in this chapter, you can control all these needs in your indoor garden and achieve optimum results.

Seedling

Flowering Burmese #5 female

Vegetative

Cannabis is a short-day plant. In nature, it flowers when autumn days are short and nights are long. Outdoors, cannabis normally grows as an annual plant, completing its life cycle within one year. A seed that is planted in the spring will grow through the summer and flower in the fall, producing more seeds.

Cannabis goes through three distinct stages of growth: seedling, vegetative, and flowering. Most varieties or strains will stay in the vegetative growth stage as long as they receive 18–24 hours of light and 6–0 hours of darkness. Most strains of cannabis will flower when they receive 12 hours of light and 12 hours of uninterrupted darkness.

Indoors you can use this knowledge to control the life cycle and harvest up to six crops a year.

Seedling Growth

Seed germination is induced with moisture, heat, and air which activate hormones within the seed. Within 24–72 hours the seed's coating splits and a white rootlet emerges and continues to grow. The Nebula seeds (right) have been germinating for 24 hours.

After three to seven days of germination, the rootlet grows downward and a sprout with seed leaves pushes upwards in search of light. Plants like the Jamaican Pearls (right) continue the seedling growth stage about a month. During this stage the seed establishes a root system and grows a stem and a few leaves. Seedlings need 16–18 hours of light to grow strong and healthy.

Vegetative Growth

Vegetative growth is maintained in this AK-47 and other strains by giving plants 18–24 hours of light every day. As the plant matures, the roots take on specialized functions of transporting and storing food. The root tips push farther and farther into the soil in search of more water and food. The delicate root hairs actually absorb water and nutrients. Delicate root hairs will dry up and die without water. They are very frail and are easily damaged by light, air, and bumbling hands if moved or exposed.

The stem also grows upward producing new buds along the stem. The central or terminal bud of this Thaitanic carries growth upward; side or lateral buds turn into branches or leaves. The stem carries water and nutrients from the roots to the growing buds, leaves, and flowers. If the stem is bound too tightly by string or other tie-downs, it will cut the flow of life-giving fluids, thereby strangling the plant. The stem also supports the plant.

Often indoor plants develop weak stems and may need to be staked up, especially during flowering. Bending and training plants also makes best use of light indoors.

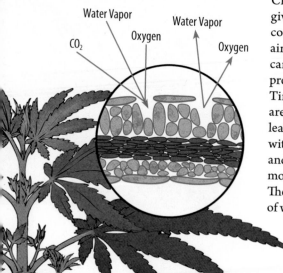

Chlorophyll (the substance that gives plants their green color) converts carbon dioxide (CO_2) from air, water, and light energy into carbohydrates and oxygen. This process is called photosynthesis. Tiny breathing pores called stomata are located on the underside of the leaf and funnel CO_2 into contact with the water. The stomata open and close to regulate the flow of moisture, preventing dehydration. The stomata also permit the outflow of water vapor and waste oxygen.

Pre-flowering

Cannabis grown from seed grows pre-flowers after the fourth week of vegetative growth. You can see a male pre-flower nub in the photo above. They generally appear between the fourth and sixth node from the bottom of the plant. Cannabis plants are normally either all male or all female. However, occasionally an intersex plant with both male and female flowers will appear. Each sex has its own distinct flowers. Pre-flowers will be either male or female. Growers remove and destroy the males (or use them for breeding stock) because they have low levels of cannabinoids (chemical components of marijuana: THC, CBD, CBN, etc.). The most desirable female plants are cultivated for their high THC content.

Intersex (aka hermaphrodite) flowers normally show up late in flowering and not at the pre-flowering stage.

Flowering

Flowering is triggered in most strains of cannabis like the Chronic bud (below) by 12 hours of darkness and 12 hours of light every 24 hours. Once flowering is induced with the 12/12 light/dark schedule, they are at peak ripeness in 7–12 weeks. Plants that developed in tropical regions often start flowering under more light and less darkness.

Female pre-flowers

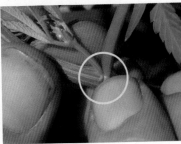

Male pre-flowers

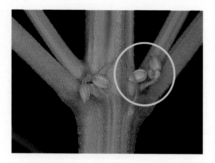

Flowering Male Plants

Male seedlings that were not removed during pre-flowering are removed as soon as male flowers are visible so that they do not pollinate females. A grower removed the Super Silver Haze plant (left) from his garden as soon as he saw the male flowers.

Flowering Female "Sinsemilla" Plants

Unpollinated female flower buds develop without seeds, known as "sinsemilla." Sinsemilla flower buds continue to swell and produce more resin while waiting for male pollen to successfully complete their life cycle. After weeks of heavy flower and cannabinoid-laden resin production, THC production peaks out and buds are ready to harvest.

Seed Crops

When both male and female flowers are in bloom, pollen from the male flower lands on the female flower, thus fertilizing it. The male dies after producing and shedding all his pollen. Seeds form and grow within the female flowers such as the seeds of the Sweet Diesel (left). You can collect the seeds roughly six to eight weeks after pollination.

Mother Plants

Select strong, healthy, potent mother plants. Give mothers 18–24 hours of light daily so they stay in the vegetative growth stage. Cut branch tips from mother plants and root them. The rooted cuttings are called "clones." Cultivating several strong, healthy mother plants is the key to having a consistent supply of all-female clones.

Clones

Cut branch tips and root them to form clones. Clones take 10–20 days to grow a strong healthy root system. Give clones 18–24 hours of light so they stay in the vegetative growth stage. Once the root system is established, transplant clones into larger containers. Now they are ready to grow for one to four weeks in the vegetative growth stage before being induced to flower.

CHAPTER 2

Security!

Security = keeping your crop secure from cops and robbers!

Avoid visits from armed policemen!

INTRODUCTION

Sadly we have to worry about security to grow a simple plant that has been on this earth since long before man set foot on it. About 70 years ago Prohibition started in the United States of America, Land of the Free. Today this crazy, paranoid prohibition has progressed and it is necessary to grow gardens in secure locations.

Security has several facets and levels. First you must restrict access to your garden. Do this by securing the perimeter around the grow house or wherever the garden is located. You will need to control everything and everybody that enters and exits the area in proximity to the garden. You can have visitors in your home, but always keep the garden under lock and key to restrict access. Make sure there are no telltale signs of growing, the most obvious of which are fragrance, light leaks, noise, and growing supplies or debris.

External forces could be tipped off to the garden's existence by your telling others about the garden; telephone conversations; tracking you home from hydroponics stores, other grow houses, or dealers' houses; lifestyle; computer data tracking; and thermal imaging devices. Choose your friends and romantic partners carefully. Most often security breaches are the result of a jealous or vindictive friend, lover, or partner. Many times these friends and partners are pressured by police to turn you in.

See Seed Ordering Security in Chapter 3.

Keep your grow room secure and safe from thieves.

Security Hit List

- Never tell anybody about any garden
- Never show your garden to anyone!
- Do not throw out any garbage that could prove that you grow
- Never have seeds or grow products sent directly to your home
- Do not visit other grow houses, wild parties, real criminals, etc.
- Take a friend's car or have a friend take you to the grow store, and go seldom

Keep your computer secure from criminal and government snoops. Check the sites

www.pgp.com/
www.pgpi.org/products/pgp/versions/freeware/
http://en.wikipedia.org/wiki/OpenPGP#OpenPGP

and search for "proxy server" at www.google.com for more information about Internet security.

Thermal Image Technology

Thermal image technology is illegal in the USA as a means to secure a search warrant, but in Canada, Holland, and other countries authorities fly grids over urban areas to look for possible growers. Nonetheless, thermal image technology is seldom a problem for small growers who use less than 2000 watts of light.

Larger growers outwit thermal imaging devices by keeping lights on during daylight hours to confuse the technology. They further safeguard their grow operation by cooling exhaust air and expelling it under a well-insulated grow house so it does not leave a heat trail. Learn more about thermal imaging at http://en.wikipedia.org/wiki/Thermography.

More Security Details

- Call grow and seed stores from a secure or remote telephone
- Pay all bills and make all purchases with cash
- Pay for mail-order merchandise with a money order
- Use a digital camera to take photos of your garden. Do not use a film camera!
- Have a guard dog
- Buy a fire extinguisher rated to put out wood, paper, grease, oil, and electrical fires
- Unload grow supplies a little bit at a time or from within a locked garage
- Put the telephone, electricity, garbage, etc., in a friend's name
- Grow in a rented home
- Eliminate light leaks
- Make Internet postings that may incriminate you from a "safe" computer via a proxy server

Electricity
- Do not steal electricity
- Electric bill—is it the same as the previous tenants?
- Ground all electrical outlets and connections
- Inspect electrical connections for signs of heat damage and repair immediately
- Keep electrical use to a reasonable amount, and keep the air clean around the house

Fragrance
- Do not let grow room air-conditioner water drain outdoors; it smells like cannabis
- Discharge odor-laden air via a roof vent or chimney
- Use a carbon filter and an ozone generator to neutralize the marijuana fragrance

Noise
- Muffle all noise from fans, ballasts, pumps, etc.
- Use insulated ducting
- Put rubber or foam fittings on all fans to reduce noise and vibrations
- Set ballasts on a noise-reducing base

Lifestyle
- Never trust anybody—friends, family, brother, sister, children, even your mother!
- Have a regular schedule and simple lifestyle
- Have a reason for extra electrical consumption
- Don't flash a large cash income. Buy large assets such as houses and cars over time
- Have a regular job and a reason for your activities
- Have few visitors and keep to yourself
- Keep a low profile and be a good neighbor and citizen
- Keep your property clean and in excellent repair
- Drive a street-legal car with no outstanding warrants on the drivers
- Pay bills on time

CHAPTER 3

Seeds and Germination

INTRODUCTION

A seed contains all the genetic characteristics of a plant. Seeds are the result of sexual propagation and contain genes from each parent, male and female. Some plants, known as hermaphrodites, bear both male and female flowers on the same plant. The genes within a seed dictate a plant's size; disease and pest resistance; root, stem, leaf, and flower production; cannabinoid levels; and many other traits. The genetic makeup of a seed is the single most important factor dictating how well a plant will grow under artificial light or natural sunlight and the levels of cannabinoids it will produce.

Weak plants are the result of weak seeds and poor growing conditions. Strong, healthy parents and proper care yield strong seeds that germinate well. Strong seeds produce healthy plants and heavy harvests. Seeds stored too long will germinate slowly and have a high rate of failure. Vigorous seeds initiate growth within seven days or sooner. Seeds that take longer than a month to germinate could always be slow and produce less.

Strong plants are the result of strong seeds and proper growing conditions.

Weak plant grown in poor conditions.

People grow seeds rather than clones because of "hybrid vigor," a phenomenon that causes F1 seeds that are the product of two true-breeding parents to grow about 25 percent stronger and bigger.

Typically, a grower who acquires 5–15 quality seeds from a reputable seed company germinates them all at once. Once germinated, the seeds are carefully planted and grown to adulthood. Normally some of the seeds will be male, some will grow slowly, and two or three seeds will grow into strong "super" females. Of these super females, one will be more robust and potent. Select this super female to be the clone mother.

Mature seeds that are hard, beige to dark brown, and spotted or mottled have the highest germination rate. Soft, pale, or green seeds are usually immature and should be avoided. Immature seeds germinate poorly and often produce sickly plants. Fresh, dry, mature seeds less than a year old sprout quickly and grow robust plants.

Order seed catalogs

Strong seeds are hard, mature, and dark.

Weak seeds are soft, immature, and pale.

Germinating and Planting Seeds

To germinate, seeds need moisture, warmth, and air (oxygen).

Moisture

Soaking seeds in water allows moisture to penetrate the protective seed shell within minutes. Moisture continues to wick in to activate the dormant hormones. In 24–72 hours, hormones activate and send signals to produce a small white rootlet (radicle).

Moisture is critical now. There must be a constant stream of moisture to transport nutrients, hormones, and water in order to carry on life processes. For best results use distilled water. Letting germinated seeds suffer moisture stress now will stunt seedling growth.

Warmth

Cannabis seeds grow best at 78°F (25°C). Low temperatures (below 70°F [21°C]) delay germination. High temperatures (above 90°F [32°C]) cause poor germination. Once germinated, move seedlings to a slightly cooler growing area and increase light levels. Avoid high temperatures and low light levels, which cause lanky growth.

Air (oxygen)

Seeds need air to germinate. Moist, soggy growing mediums will cut off oxygen supplies and the seed will literally drown. Planting seeds too deeply also causes poor germination. Seedlings do not have enough stored energy to force through too much soil before sprouting. Plant seeds twice as deep as the width of the seed. For example, plant a 0.125-inch (0.3 mm) seed 0.25-inch (6 mm) deep.

TIMELINE FOR GERMINATING SEEDS	
At 55–72 hours	Water is absorbed and root tip (radicle) is visible
At 10–14 days	First roots become visible
At 21–30 days	At least half of seeds are rooted by day 21

- Seeds not rooted by day 30 will probably grow slowly
- Once seeds are rooted, cell growth accelerates; stem, foliage, and roots develop quickly
- Seedlings develop into full vegetative growth within four to six weeks of germination

Cannabis Strains

Technically and legally, all cannabis, whether rope or dope, is classified as *Cannabis sativa*. Regardless of origin, all cannabis is considered *Cannabis sativa* (*C. sativa*) under international law. However, according to *Hemp Diseases and Pests*, Dr. J. M. McPartland, R. C. Clarke, and D. P. Watson, (CAB International), *Cannabis sativa* can be further classified as: *Cannabis sativa* (= *C. sativa* var. *sativa*), *Cannabis indica* (= *C. sativa* var. *indica*), *Cannabis ruderalis* (= *C. sativa* var. *spontanea*), *Cannabis afghanica* (= *C. sativa* var. *afghanica*). Each has distinct growth patterns, look, smell, taste, etc.

Most popular strains of cannabis are a combination of two or more of the following: *C. sativa*, *C. indica*, *C. ruderalis*, and *C. afghanica*. But there are also many seeds with the genes from just one of the below.

Afghanica Afghani has wide leaves and is often confused with *indica* strains.

Ruderalis Lowryder female plant

Sativa Neville's Haze female plant

Indica Sensi Star female plant

Step-by-Step: Germination and Planting

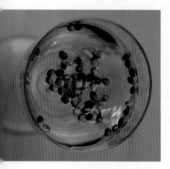  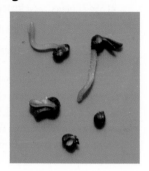

STEP ONE: Day 1

Presoak seeds in a glass of plain (distilled) water for 24 hours. Do not soak longer or they could rot. At first seeds will float on top of the water. As water penetrates they sink to the bottom.

Within a few hours, seeds will sink to the bottom of the container. Seeds found floating the following day are probably not viable.

A small, white rootlet often emerges from strong viable seeds.

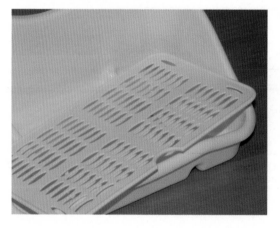

STEP TWO: Day 2

Use a dinner plate or a small container with a grate. A grate lets excess water drain away. If using a plate, tip it to drain off excess water.

Set a paper towel or cheesecloth on the plate or grate and moisten it with distilled water until saturated.

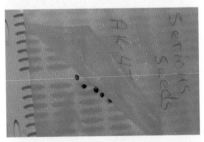

Pour the water out of the glass and place the seeds on the moist paper towels and cover the seeds with three more moist paper towels.

Drain off all excess water and put the moist seeds in a shadowy, warm location (70°–90°F, [21°–32°C]). The top of a refrigerator is ideal. Check daily and keep evenly moist but not soggy. Do not let seeds dry out or let water stand so oxygen is cut off to seeds. Let excess water drain away freely.

NOTE: Prevent fungal attacks by watering with a mild two-percent bleach solution.

STEP THREE: Days 5–8

Once seeds have sprouted and the white sprout is visible, they are ready to be moved into the growing medium. Seeds that do not show a white rootlet now may never germinate. Do not throw them out, plant them. But such seeds might never germinate, and if they grow they could turn into weak plants.

STEP FOUR: Days 5–8

Prepare a seed flat, Jiffy or rockwool cubes, etc. for planting
sprouted seeds. Fill the seed flat with a store-bought seedling
mix or make your own 50/50 mix of fine perlite and peat moss
or coco peat.

Water the mix in the flat with plain
water until it is completely saturated; water should run freely from
the drainage holes in the bottom
when the medium is saturated.

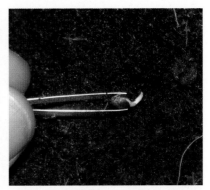

Seedlings do not have enough stored energy to force through too much soil before sprouting. Plant seeds twice as deep as the width of the seed. For example, plant an eighth-inch (3 mm) seed 0.25-inch (6 mm) deep. Make small indent about 0.25-inch (6 mm) in the growing medium, one for each seed in individual containers.

Use tweezers and carefully remove each sprouted seed and set it in the premade planting hole. Take care not to expose the tender rootlet to prolonged intense light or air. Point the white root downward.

Cover the sprouted seed with a 0.25-inch (6 mm) layer of fine, moist planting mix.

Once covered, gently press the soil into firm contact with the sprouted seed.

Once planted, set the flat or rooting cubes of sprouted seedlings under the lamp. The photo above shows clones
on the left and seedlings on the right.

Seeds set inside rockwool blocks often heave up and out.
Germinate seeds before planting and make sure the white
rootlet is at least 0.5-inch (1.5 cm) long to avoid this
common problem.

STEP FIVE: Days 10–14

In four to six days after planting, most of the seeds will have broken through the planting mix or emerged from the root cube.

Within a couple of days of emerging, the first smooth, non-serrated cotyledon leaves emerge. Some seedlings will show their first signs of "true leaves" with the classic cannabis serrations and pointed tips.

After seven to ten days, all the seedlings will have cotyledon leaves and many will have their first set of true leaves.

In 10 to 14 days all the seedlings should have true leaves that are the same size or larger than cotyledons.

Some growers apply a mild (quarter-strength) fertilizer, but it is not necessary for another week. Most important now is to keep the soil evenly moist.

STEP SIX: Days 21–30

Start feeding two to four weeks after seedlings have sprouted. Some growers wait until leaves yellow to begin feeding. Use a mild quarter-strength solution. If yellowing persists, give seedlings a little more fertilizer.

STEP SEVEN: Days 21–30

Peat pellets or root cubes (both seedlings and clones) may be transplanted in two to three weeks or when the roots show through the sides. Feed with a dilute, quarter-strength fertilizer solution.

STEP EIGHT: Days 26–30

Grow seedlings and clones under light fluorescent or dim HID light for the next couple of weeks, until they have two to three sets of true leaves. This is a critical time for plants, and they need extremely close attention. Do not let them dry out!

Potential Problems

Too much or too little light coupled with overwatering or underwatering are the main reasons for poor seedling growth. This sickly freak trifoliate seedling is the result of dodgy genetics as well.

Overwatering and underwatering are the biggest obstacles most growers face when germinating seeds and growing seedlings. Keep the soil uniformly moist, not waterlogged. Do not let the growing medium's surface dry for long. Keep it evenly moist. Setting root cubes or planting flats on a grate allows good drainage. A shallow flat or planter with a heat pad underneath may require daily watering, while a deep, one-gallon pot will need watering every three days or more. A properly watered flat of rockwool cubes needs water every three to five days when sprouting seeds. When the surface is dry (0.25-inch [6 mm] deep) it is time to water. Remember, there are few roots to absorb the water early in life, and they are very delicate.

Seeds do not need any extra hormones to germinate. Household water contains enough dissolved solids (food) to nourish seeds through their first few weeks of life. Supplemental nutrients often disrupt internal chemistry.

Underwatered seedling with a purple stem demonstrates toxic nutrient accumulation. This seedling is also a genetically unstable trifoliate with three sets of leaves and should be culled out.

Soggy overwatered soil causes many problems.

How to Obtain Seeds

Get seeds from a grower who developed them. This is an excellent option because the grower usually knows the strain he is growing well and can tell you many details about growing it. Most such growers can also tell you about the qualities of the plant—taste, aroma, and high.

Find seeds in a bag of buds. Bag-seeds are okay because you will know more or less what the taste, aroma, and high of the final product will be like. However, you will not know the growth characteristics of the plant, and the plant will not be genetically stable. Often the seed will grow into a plant that has only some traits of the parents. It could also have intersex (hermaphrodite) tendencies.

Order seeds via mail order or Internet. There are many seed shops that sell on-line listed under Find Seed Sellers Here on page 40. Also check cannabis web site forums for more information and recommendations.

Before you buy anything, send the seed company an e-mail with some questions and see how long it takes them to respond. A good seed company will respond in one to two business days with good answers to your questions. If you do not get a response, do not order!

You may prefer to order from a company you can contact by telephone (see note under Seed Ordering Security on page 40). Speak to a qualified representative who will provide good answers to your questions. Companies with an e-mail address and web site are usually okay to order from, but make sure they answer your e-mails promptly. Always call several companies and ask them specific questions about the strains they sell.

Packaging is important. Seeds are easily crushed, and packaging must protect them from damage. Many seed companies place seeds inside the channels of corrugated plastic (see photo left of filling seed packages at Dutch Passion). The corrugated plastic is then placed inside an envelope and mailed. The volume of first class mail is great, and all sorting is done mechanically.

Letters under one ounce (28 grams) are not opened. Occasionally the Postal service will find such a seed shipment. When they do, they send a letter to the recipient stating they have confiscated the seeds. No further action is taken.

Caution! Some seed merchants do not tell the truth about their seed stock. They sell you seeds that are not what they advertise them to be. Other companies take your money and do not ship the seeds. It is easy to overcome such problems with a little homework. Always check Greenman's site, www.seedbankupdate.com, for current information on seed banks. The site also lists seed banks that do not advertise in catalogs. Seed sellers are rated with one to four stars, depending on the quality and services they offer. Greenman gives security, shipping, and payment terms as well as a rating for customer complaints including an "X" rating for rip-offs as well as many other grievances.

Purchase seeds personally at a shop. Seeds are available at shops in many countries. Stores in Canada, Holland, Italy, Spain, Switzerland, United Kingdom, and several Central European countries sell seeds publicly. You can walk right in and buy them. Find such seed stores at the web sites listed by the magazines and cannabis fair guides on the following page. When you talk personally with a seed merchant, you get exact information and can ask as many questions as you want. Often the salesperson has personal stories about favorite strains.

QUESTIONS
1. How are seeds shipped in a stealth package?
2. When will seeds be shipped?
3. How are seeds packaged?
4. Are seeds in stock?
5. How long does the average order take to arrive?
6. What happens if seeds are lost?
7. Do you ship worldwide?

Green Man's Seedbank Update

This site is dedicated to medical marijuana users and all those who can use the information legally. Here you will find a list of honest seedbanks with ratings based on reports from buyers of cannabis seeds. This service has been in existence since Jan 1998.

- The monthly update Seedbank listings with this month's commentary.
- Strains a list of cannabis strains with descriptions.
- ozone generator Plans for a home built ozone generator to combat odors
- Cure Ways to cure your crop and give flavors
- Links Grow information and pot friendly businesses
- New New and unrated seedbanks
- Aero clonerInstructions for a cheap do it yourself aerocloner
- New book by Jorge Cervantes

www.seedbankupdate.com

Find Seed Sellers Here

Canada
www.hightimes.com
www.cannabisculture.com
www.skunkmagazine.com

Holland
www.highlife.nl

Italy
www.highlife.nl
www.dolcevitaonline.it
www.softsecrets.com

Spain
www.highlife.nl
www.canamo.net
www.softsecrets.com

Switzerland
www.cannatrade.ch

United Kingdom
www.softsecrets.com
www.theredeyeexpress.co.uk
www.weedworld.co.uk

USA
www.hightimes.com
Many medical marijuana
clubs and dispensaries in
California and other states
where medical marijuana is
legal sell seeds. Search
"medical cannabis club" on
www.google.com.

Seed Ordering Security

- Pay with a money order, cash, or a business credit card with a business address to minimize on-line ordering risks. Ask seed vendor to destroy your payment information as soon as your order is processed.
- Ship seeds to a real address and name. Use some initials in the name and address, and misspell the name but still make it deliverable.
- Ship seeds to a third party—friend, family member, business, etc. They do not need to know what is in the package. Ask them not to open the package.
- Do not have seeds shipped to the same address where your garden is located
- Do not have packages sent that require a signature
- Use a public e-mail address when ordering. Count on your e-mails being saved somewhere. Do not use this e-mail for other purposes.
- Increase security by using a proxy server to hide your computer's IP address. Learn more about proxy servers by searching for "proxy server security" on www.google.com.
- Patience is a virtue. International shipments take longer than domestic shipments. Wait several days longer before you start searching for the shipment. Do not telephone or e-mail vendor until a reasonable time has passed.

Many national governments monitor all international telephone calls. Use a telephone card and call from a public telephone or one that cannot be traced back to you.

If you live in a country where seeds are illegal, call from a public telephone and use a calling card. Do not call the seed company from a telephone located at a grow house. Even if you are a medical marijuana grower in the United States of America, the seeds must pass the US border and federal law applies.

Seized Seeds: Note for USA Citizens

If Customs seizes your order of seeds, they will send you a note informing you of that fact. We have never heard a report of a law enforcement official showing up at the door of a seed buyer.

You can see an actual letter at the site www.onlinepot.org and http://www. onlinepot.org/ mailing_scams/ badboyletter.htm. You will receive the letter with the dreaded green tape that says "Opened by US Customs."

NOTICE OF REMOVAL

This shipment contained item(s) that were determined to be an illegal importation. The US Customs Service has the responsibility to intercept and seize illegal items when they are attempted to be brought into the United States by any means. Accordingly, the items(s) were removed from the shipment and seized by the US Customs Service. The remaining items in this shipment are being forwarded on to you as they are not considered to be an importation contrary to US Customs and/or related laws.

If you have any questions regarding the US Customs seizure, contact:

PORT DIRECTOR OF CUSTOMS
FINES, PENALTIES, AND FORFEITURES
STREET ADDRESS
CITY, STATE AND ZIP CODE

Case number xxxxxxxxxxxx

Seed Quantities and Pricing

Seeds are generally sold in packages of 5, 10, and 15. Prices range from about $3 to $30 USD per seed. Often less expensive seeds are perfectly adequate for many growers' needs and desires. More expensive seeds are usually more stable and extra care has been taken to produce them. Furthermore, expensive seeds are often winners of recent cannabis cups or are more difficult to produce. My preference is to purchase seeds that are in the middle price range. Unless feminized, always purchase packages of 10–15 seeds, because the odds are that 50 percent of the seeds will be female and the other half male. Of the desired female seeds, some will show more desirable characteristics than others.

Feminized Seeds

Feminized seeds are becoming very popular world-wide. When grown in a stress-free environment virtually all feminized seeds grow into female plants. They are more expensive than "normal" seeds. Normal seeds generally yield a 50/50 mix of male and female plants. Male plants are weeded out and female seeds are harvested.

Receiving Seeds

Check seeds to ensure none are crushed. If seeds came in a see-through bag, do not open it. Call or e-mail the seller immediately to explain the problem. If one or a few are crushed, return all seeds for replacement.

If you are not going to plant the seeds immediately, remove them and keep them from the original package. Keep seeds dry or they might start to germinate. Place them in a small dark vial or film canister with a dry packet of silicone, the kind you find in electronics packages. Label the crush-proof container before you place the seeds inside.

Storing Seeds

Store seeds in a cool, dark, dry place. See Receiving Seeds, page 42. Make sure to label containers! Some seeds will remain viable for five years or longer when stored properly. When 50 percent of the stored seeds do not germinate, the average storage life is over. But seeds a year old or older often take longer to sprout and have a lower rate of germination. Seeds store for a long time when humidity is less than 5 percent and temperature is 35°–41°F (2°–5°C).

Seedlings

During seedling growth, the root system grows rapidly while green aboveground growth is slow. Water and heat are critical at this point of development. The new, fragile root system is very small and requires a small but constant supply of water and warmth. Too much water will drown roots, often leading to root rot and damping-off (rotting at the soil line). Lack of water will cause the developing root system to dry up. As the seedlings mature, some will grow faster, stronger, and appear healthier in general. A little heat now will help nurture small seedlings to a strong start. Other seeds will sprout slowly and be weak and leggy. Most growers cull sickly, weak plants during the third to fifth week of growth, and focus attention on the remaining strong survivors.

Speed root growth by keeping the soil 2°–5°F (1°–2°C) warmer than the ambient air temperature. Ideally the ambient air temperature should be 75°C (24°C) and the growing medium temperature 77°–80°C (25°–27°C). Use heating cables or mat to raise the temperature of the growing medium.

If you have just a few seedlings, you may want to save weak, slow-growing plants. Baby such small plants along and let them grow longer until they catch up with the others before moving them into the next stage of growth.

Seedlings need at least 16 hours of light daily. Many growers give seedlings 18–24 hours of light per day so they will grow as fast as possible. Seedlings that receive 16 hours of light and 8 hours of darkness tend to grow more female plants.

Seedlings require less intense light now and grow well under fluorescent tubes or compact fluorescent lamps (CFLs) for the first two to three weeks. Keep fluorescent lamps two to six inches above seedlings and CFLs 12–18 inches (30–45 cm) above foliage.

Metal halide or HP sodium HID lights can be used to grow
seedlings. Growers prefer metal halides because the color
spectrum of HP sodium lamps tends to make seedlings stretch
between branch internodes. Keep HIDs three to four feet
(90–120 cm) above seedlings for best growth.

The seedling stage is over when
rapid foliage growth starts. Rapid
growth above ground is the beginning of the vegetative growth stage.
Plants need more room to grow;
transplanting into a larger container
hastens development.

Transplanting Seedlings

If you are growing a few seedlings, they are easier to maintain in bigger containers. This example shows how to transplant a small seedling grown in a rockwool cube into a 4-inch (12 cm) container full of potting soil.

1 Carefully remove the seedling in the moist rockwool block from the seedling container.

2 Place the rockwool cube in a premade hole in the container of potting soil or soilless mix.

3 Add more soil to cover the rockwool cube. Rockwool, Oasis, peat pots, etc. hold more water than most soils and soilless mixes. It is very important to cover them when transplanting. If the cube is left uncovered, roots tend to stay in the root cube and not grow into the soil.

4 Here is the same seedling near the end of the seedling growth stage.

CHAPTER 4
Vegetative Growth

INTRODUCTION

Cannabis enters the vegetative growth stage after four to six weeks of seedling growth.* Vegetative growth is maintained in most strains with 16–24 hours of light daily. Plants grow faster when they receive more hours of light. Marijuana will continue vegetative growth a year or longer (theoretically forever) as long as it receives 18–24 hours of light every day.

During the vegetative stage, green leafy growth is rapid. Healthy plants will grow an inch or more daily. Strong, fast vegetative growth is essential for a heavy harvest. Plants that are stunted now should not be induced to flower because they will yield much less. Hold them back until they are stronger.

Proper levels of nutrients are important for fast-growing vegetative plants. Make sure you are following the manufacturer's recommended dosage when fertilizing. Some plants can take much more fertilizer than others.

*In general, seedlings grow 4-5 weeks and 2 weeks of vegetative growth for a total of 5-6 weeks before being moved into the flowering room.

In general pure *sativa* and *sativa*-dominant strains require less fertilizer. The photo at left is a good example of a Haze strain that received very little fertilizer and suffered from overfertilization. One of the best ways to learn a strain's fertilizer tolerance is to experiment so that you will know exactly how much fertilizer this specific strain needs.

In general pure *indica* and *indica*-dominant strains can take higher doses of fertilizer. The photo at left is a good example of an *indica* strain that received high doses of fertilizer before it started showing signs of overfertilization. Check with seed sellers and Internet forums to learn more about which strains can take high and low doses of fertilizers. Check *Marijuana Horticulture: The Indoor/Outdoor Medical Grower's Bible* for more specific information on fertilizer dosage and photos of under- and overfertilized plants.

When to Induce Flowering

After four to five weeks of vegetative growth, plants grow early male or female pre-flowers. Once these pre-flowers appear, plants are ready to enter the flowering growth stage. To learn more about pre-flowering and what they look like, see Chapter 5: Pre-flowering.

Indoors you can control the life cycle of cannabis with light and dark. This light and dark cycle is called the photoperiod. Cannabis stays in the vegetative growth stage as long as it receives 18–24 hours of light. Flowering is induced with 12 hours of *uninterrupted* darkness and 12 hours of light per day. The 12/12 day/night photoperiod triggers most strains of cannabis to flower.

The vegetative growth stage is only two to four weeks long in most strains when grown indoors. Plants should be from 12–18 inches (30–45 cm) at the end of vegetative growth. If they are taller, artificial light will not be able to penetrate the foliage to the bottom.

Plants will need to be flushed at the end of the vegetative growth stage and possibly once in between after three weeks. I like to flush plants with three times the amount of weak fertilizer solution as the amount of soil or soilless mix in the container. This will flush or leach out all the extra built up toxic fertilizer salts in the growing medium.

Mother plants (see Chapter 7) enjoy a longer life from six months and occasionally as long as several years. Once a plant's sex is determined at pre-flowering, it can become a mother, clone, or breeding male.

CHAPTER 5

Pre-flowering

INTRODUCTION

Marijuana is a dioecious plant, being either male (right, pollen producing) or female (center right, ovule and seed producing). However, intersex (aka hermaphrodite or bisexual) plants with both male and female flowers can also occur. See Intersex or Hermaphrodite Flowers in Chapter 6: Flowering for more information.

Pre-flowers are the first sign of a plant's sex. The pre-flowers grow at branch internodes just behind the leaf spur or stipule about the fourth week of vegetative growth, when the plant is six to eight weeks old. This is the point of sexual maturity, the first sign a plant is preparing for flowering—the next stage in life.

You can see pre-flowers with the naked eye, but a 10x to 30x magnifier will make viewing easier. You can accurately determine plant sex after eight weeks. Using this method, you can distinguish sex before inducing flowering.

Plants grown from seed under an 18/6 day/night photoperiod will generally show pre-flowers before plants that are given a 24/0 day/night photoperiod. Once pre-flowers are distinguishable as male or female, plants can be induced to flower with a 12/12 day/night photoperiod.

Male

Female

Female pre-flowers

Male Pre-flowering

The little nub is a male pre-flower starting to grow.

Male pre-flowers are normally visible when plants are six to eight weeks old, after the fourth week of vegetative growth. The pre-flowers emerge behind the stipule at the fourth to fifth branch internodes and generally do not turn into full flowers.

Another view of the little nub that will turn into a male flower.

Early male flowers are easy to spot with the naked eye. They are located at branch internodes. Male pollen sacks hang like little balls. Each pollen sac has enough pollen to pollinate all the females in the average grow room.

Remove and destroy male plants grown from seed as soon as you can verify male pre-flowers. Removing male plants now will virtually ensure an all-female crop of sinsemilla.

Female Pre-flowering

Female calyx formation initiates about the fourth week of vegetative growth when they develop female pre-flowers. The appearance of pre-flowers does not depend upon photoperiod. It occurs when a plant is old enough to show signs of sexual maturity, about six to eight weeks from seed germination. The pre-flowers emerge behind the stipule at the fourth to fifth branch internodes.

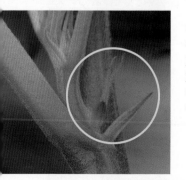

A pre-flower looks like a regular female flower; most have a pair of white fuzzy pistils. Pistils normally emerge after the light green seed bract part of the pre-flower has formed. Wait until pistils have formed to ensure the plant is a female and not a male. The pre-flowering stage lasts from one to two weeks.

Plants grown from seed under an 18/6 day/night photoperiod will usually show pronounced pre-flowers before plants given a 24/0 day/night photoperiod. And, under a 16/8 day/night regimen pre-flowers show more quickly and are often more pronounced. Once pre-flowers are distinguishable as female, plants can be induced to flower with a 12/12 day/night photoperiod.

Always wait to induce flowering until after pre-flowers appear. Inducing flowering with 12 hours of uninterrupted darkness and 12 hours of light before pre-flowers develop will stress the plant. This stress could cause odd growth, and plants might grow into hermaph-rodites. Inducing flowering before pre-flowers form will not speed flowering. Flowering will occur about the same time as if you had waited for pre-flowers to show!

Vegetative seedlings are now ready to start flowering. Male and female flowers will form and are easy to see. This garden is full of females that have been flowering for three weeks.

CHAPTER 6

Flowering

INTRODUCTION

Cannabis is an annual plant that normally produces seeds to successfully complete its life cycle. Marijuana is a dioecious plant, being either male (pollen-producing) or female (ovule- and seed-producing). However, intersex (aka hermaphrodite or bisexual) plants with both male and female flowers can also occur.

Male plant with pollen-producing flowers

Female plant with unfertilized pollen-producing flowers

Intersex plant with both male and female flowers

In nature, cannabis flowers in the fall, after the long days of summer. The long nights and short days of autumn signal marijuana to start flowering. Plants are normally either male or female.

Growth patterns and chemistry change during flowering: stems elongate; leaves grow progressively fewer blades; cannabinoid production slows at first, then accelerates; and flower formation is rapid at first, then slows. Nutrient needs change as growth stages change. Plants focus on flower production rather than vegetative growth. Green leafy growth, requiring much nitrogen, slows. Phosphorus and potassium uptake increase to promote floral formation. Shortly before the flowering stage, growers change to a "super bloom" fertilizer formula with less nitrogen and more potassium and phosphorus. Always flush or leach soil with water two to three days before changing to the flowering fertilizer.

When flowers are full of ripe, mature seeds, the female will die, having successfully completed her life cycle. The male completes his life cycle and dies after producing and dispersing all his pollen into the wind, in search of receptive female pistils.

Induce flowering indoors by giving plants more hours of total darkness and fewer hours of light. Give cannabis 12 hours of *uninterrupted* darkness and 12 hours of light to induce visible signs of flowering in two weeks or less. This program is effective in all but the latest-blooming pure *sativa* strains.

Often, when using low-nitrogen, high-phosphorus and potassium bloom formulas, large older leaves yellow or turn purple during flowering. Such fertilizers make buds swell with resinous growth.

Water intake of flowering plants is usually somewhat less than during the vegetative stage. Adequate water during flowering is important for plants to carry on internal chemistry and resin production. Withholding water to "stress" a plant will actually stunt growth and diminish yield.

Inducing flowering in cannabis grown from seed with a 12/12 day/night photoperiod will cause plants to show sex, male (above) or female. Once the sex of the plant is guaranteed, males are almost always harvested before they shed pollen, and females are coaxed into higher yields. Once the photoperiod is set, disrupting it will cause plants to suffer stress. If they suffer enough stress, hermaphrodite tendencies increase.

Male Flowering

When given a 12/12 day/night photoperiod, male cannabis reaches maturity and flowers one to two weeks before females. However, male plants do not necessarily need a 12/12 day/night photoperiod to grow flowers and shed pollen. Some male plants flower under long days and short nights as well, but these generally produce fewer flowers.

Early male flowers that are not open or dispersing pollen

Open male flowers that are dispersing pollen

Once male calyxes show, pollen develops quickly and can disperse within a very short time. There is always a flower sack that opens early and sheds pollen, often within 24 hours or less! To avoid pollination problems, remove males as soon as they are distinguished. If growing male plants, always isolate them from females, to prevent accidental pollination.

This male was allowed to mature completely and disperse its pollen. When you decide to let male plants mature to shed pollen on receptive females, make sure to keep the male in another room and as far as possible from female plants that you do not want pollinated.

Blue Mistic

Female Flowering

Female cannabis is prized for heavy, potent resin production and weighty flower yield. Ideal female plants grow squat and bushy with branches close together on the stem and dense foliage on branches. In most strains, the first signs of female flowers appear one to three weeks after inducing flowering with the 12-hour photoperiod.

Female flowers initially appear near the top of the terminal bud and gradually develop on lower branches starting at the tips and moving downward. Flowers have two small one-quarter- to one-half-inch (6–12 mm) fuzzy white hairs called "pistils" that form a V. The set of pistils is attached at the base to an ovule, which is contained in a light-green pod called a "calyx." Pistil-packed calyxes form dense clusters or buds along stems. A cluster of buds is often called a "top" or "cola." The masses of calyxes develop rapidly for the first four or five weeks, after which they grow at a slower rate. Buds put on much of their harvest weight as they swell during the last two or three weeks of growth. Pure *sativas*, including Thai varieties, can flower for four months or longer! Once the ovule has been fertilized by male pollen, rapid calyx formation and resin production slow, and seed growth starts.

Holland Hope

Power Plant

Sinsemilla Flowering

Sinsemilla (pronounced sin·seh·mee·yah) is derived from two Spanish words: "sin" = without and "semilla" = seed. Sinsemilla is the word that describes flowering female cannabis tops that have *not* been fertilized by male pollen.

Highly prized sinsemilla buds are the most potent part of any strain, with a proportionately large volume of THC per flower bud. When females' flowering is at their peak, pistils swell and swell. Soon they change in color, most often from white to amber and, eventually, to reddish-brown.

Trichome Technologies

Burmese #3

Sinsemilla is all smoke with no seeds! Unpollinated female plants continue to flower until calyx formation and resin production peak out—six to ten weeks after turning the lights to 12 hours. During six to ten weeks of flowering, calyxes develop and swell along the stem, yielding more high-quality buds than pollinated, seeded flowers.

Make any female marijuana sinsemilla by removing male plants as soon as they are identified. Removing males virtually guarantees that male pollen will not fertilize female pistils, but sometimes premature male flowers shed a few early grains of pollen. Sometimes an intersex (hermaphrodite) with a few male flowers will sprout on a predominately female plant. Pollen dispersed from wild or cultivated male cannabis plants could also be floating in the air.

Intersex or Hermaphrodite Flowers

Intersex or hermaphrodite flowers may occur, sometimes near the end of the blooming cycle, though occasionally they appear earlier. Plants that flower past peak potency are most prone to show intersex flowers. Intersex plants are more common in some strains.

CHAPTER 7

Clones and Mother Plants

INTRODUCTION

Making clones is the most efficient and productive means of cannabis propagation for most growers. A clone is a branch tip cut from a (female) mother marijuana plant that has been planted and has grown roots. Female clones can be induced to flower as soon as they have a strong root system and are 6–18 inches (15–45 cm) tall. A crop of clones can be harvested in about three months. When planted from seed, crops take four to five months to mature. And unless you planted feminized seed (See Chapter 3: Seeds and Germination) about half of the plants will be undesirable males. Clones are not available by mail order. You must grow them yourself or get them from a grower or medical marijuana cooperative.

Induce clones to flower when they are 6–18 inches (15–45 cm) tall to make most efficient use of HID light. Short crops of clones in small containers are much easier to move and maintain than big plants in big containers.

Well-illuminated, strong clones grow fast and have less chance of being affected by pests and diseases. Fast-growing clones develop more quickly than spider mites can reproduce. By the time a spider mite infestation is noticed and sprayed, the plants are a few weeks from harvest. Clones are also easy to submerge in a miticide when small.

Mother Plants

Any plant can be cloned, regardless of age or growth stage. Take clones from mother plants that are at least two months old. Plants cloned before they are two months old may develop unevenly and grow slowly. Clones taken from flowering plants root quickly but require a month or longer to revert back to vegetative growth. Such rejuvenated clones occasionally flower prematurely, and buds are more prone to pests and diseases.

Keep several vegetative mother plants for a consistent source of cloning stock. Start new mothers from seed every year. Give mother plants 18–24 hours of light per day to maintain fast growth. For best results, give mothers about ten percent less nitrogen, because less nitrogen promotes rooting in clones.

A female plant will reproduce 100 percent females, all exactly like the mother. When grown in the exact same environment, clones from the same mother look alike. But the same clones subjected to distinct environments in different grow rooms will often look different.

Get Ready to Take Clones

Clones go through an enormous transformation when they change from a severed growing tip to a rooted plant, their entire chemistry changes. The stem that once grew leaves must now grow roots to survive. Clones are at their most vulnerable point in life when they are cut from the mother and forced to grow roots.

While rooting, clones require a minimum of nitrogen and increased levels of phosphorus to promote root growth. Avoid spraying during rooting because it creates extra stress. With good instruction and a little experience, you can achieve a consistent 100 percent clone survival rate. Large cuttings with large stems grow roots slower than small clones with small stems, and are more prone to diseases. Thin-stemmed small clones with few leaves root faster than big leafy cuttings because there are no roots to absorb water and supply moisture to foliage. A small amount of leaf space is all that is necessary to supply enough energy for root growth.

Some cuttings may wilt but regain rigidity in a few days. Older leaves may turn light green; growth slows as nitrogen is used and carbohydrates build. Carbohydrate and (rooting) hormonal content is highest in lower, older, more mature branches. A rigid branch that folds over quickly when bent is a good sign of high carbohydrate content.

Always make sure there is plenty of air in the rooting medium to stimulate root growth. Do not overwater clones. Keep the rooting medium evenly moist. Do not let it get soggy. Any kind of stress disrupts hormones and slows rapid growth.

Clones root well within a pH range of 5–6. Aeroponic clone gardens normally do best with a pH of 5–5.5.

Disinfect all tools and working surfaces to kill bacteria, fungi, viruses, and other diseases already present. Use sharp scissors, razor, or razor blade dipped in alcohol, vinegar, or bleach (five to ten percent solution). Wash your hands thoroughly beforehand.

Get all cloning supplies ready before you start to take clones.

Make sure to have all cloning supplies within arm's reach—rooting cubes, hormone, razor or scissors, humidity dome, etc.—before you start to take clones.

Here is a shot of the root systems in the aeroponic system after a few days of rooting.

There are many different "clone machines" available such as this aeroponic model that make cloning quick and easy.

expanded clay pellets

Oasis® root cubes

rockwool

soilless mix

Jiffy pot

Rooting Mediums

Set cut stems in rockwool, Jiffy (peat), Oasis root cubes, or fine soilless mix. All cubes are convenient and easy to transplant. Some growers report rockwool cubes stay too wet to make clones. Other growers love them. You can also use small containers or nursery flats full of coarse washed sand, fine vermiculite, soilless mix, or, if nothing else is available, fine potting soil.

Fill rockwool tray with water, pH 5–6.

The growing medium must drain very well to withstand heavy leaching without becoming waterlogged.

Rooting Hormones

Rooting hormones help initiate roots and are available in liquid, gel, or powder form. Use only products that are approved for human consumption and use before expiration date. As soon as cuttings are taken, clones start sending natural rooting hormones to the wound and arrive in full force in about a week. The artificial rooting hormone fills the need until natural hormones take over. Apply any rooting hormone containing Indolebutyric Acid (IBA) only once. If exceeded in concentration or duration, IBA applications impair root formation.

Liquid rooting hormones penetrate stems evenly and are the most versatile and consistent. They can be mixed in different concentrations. Always mix the most dilute concentration for softwood cannabis cuttings.

Gels are easy to use and practical. Gels keep root-inducing hormones evenly distributed along the subterranean stem. Insoluble gels hold and stay with the stem longer than liquids or powders.

Powdered rooting hormones do not stick to stems evenly, penetrate poorly, encourage uneven root growth, and yield a lower survival rate.

Clones root fastest and strongest with

- 18–24 hours of fluorescent light. Keep the lamps two to six inches (5–15 cm) above clones.
- Growing medium at 80°F (27°C) and ambient-air temperature 5°F (2°C) cooler. Set clones on a heating mat or cables to control the rooting medium temperature.
- Humidity levels of 95 to 100 percent the first two days and gradually reduced to 85 percent over the next seven days. Cover clones with a humidity dome. Mist cuttings with water to slow moisture loss through leaves and cool foliage. A fogger in the cloning room will ensure humidity stays above 95 percent.
- No tugging on clones to see if they are rooted. Roots should be visible through rooting cubes in one to three weeks.
- No fertilizer on clones or seedlings the first week or two of growth.

Step-by-Step: Cloning

STEP ONE

Carefully select a strong healthy (female) mother plant that is at least two months old. Do not take clones from a sick pest- or disease-infested or flowering mother.

NOTE: If the strain is difficult to clone, flush the soil with two gallons (8 L) of water for each gallon (4 L) of soil every day for a week before taking clones to wash nitrogen from the plant and soil. Take clones from lower rigid branches. Drainage must be good. Do not add fertilizer.

STEP TWO

Use a sharp disinfected blade or scissors to make a 45-degree cut across firm, healthy 0.125–0.25- inch-wide (3–6 mm) growth. When cutting, make the slice halfway between the sets of nodes. The new clones should be two to four inches (3–5 cm) long. Be careful not to crush the end of the stem where cutting.

STEP THREE

Carefully trim off two or three sets of lower leaves. Cut them off at the nodes where they meet the stem. Clones root very well when there are one or two sets of trimmed nodes belowground and two sets of leaves above the soil line. While taking clones, hold cuttings in a glass of water until you are ready to dip in hormone and plant.

STEP FOUR

Cut leaves in half to lower transpiration surface and to keep them from overlapping. Moisture that could promote fungus is often trapped between overlapping leaves.

Gather leaves in your hand and use a pair of scissors to cut the leaves in half. This will allow less surface area for the plants to breathe, but will still keep foliage on the plant. Cutting leaves like this will keep them up off the ground, which helps prevent rot and disease.

STEP FIVE

Choose a rooting medium (see Rooting Mediums, page 64). Saturate the medium or root cubes with water. Use an unsharpened pencil, chop stick, nail, etc., to make a hole in the rooting medium, a little larger than the stem of the clone. The hole should stop about one-half inch (1.5 cm) from the bottom of the container to allow for root growth.

STEP SIX:
Using Liquid Rooting Hormone

Use a rooting hormone (see Rooting Hormones, page 65). Always read and comply with the directions. Pour a small portion of the rooting hormone into another container before using so you do not contaminate the original container.

Mix the liquid rooting hormone (if necessary) just before using. Use the dilution ratio for softwood cuttings. Swirl each cutting in the hormone solution for 5–15 seconds. Make sure the liquid penetrates the entire stem evenly. Place the cuttings in the hole in the rooting medium. Pack rooting medium gently around the stem.

Dip stem in rooting hormone liquid.

Put hormone-covered stem into pre-made hole in rooting medium.

Press hole closed so that growing medium comes into firm contact with stem.

Dip stem in rooting hormone gel.

STEP SIX:
Using Gel Rooting Hormone

Dip stem in gel as per instructions. Make sure the part that will go underground is covered evenly with gel. When planting, take special care to gently pack soil into place.

Put hormone-covered stem into pre-made hole in rooting medium.

Press hole closed so that growing medium comes into firm contact with stem.

STEP SIX: Using Powdered Rooting Hormone

Roll stem in rooting powder so that the underground part is covered evenly. When planting, take special care to gently pack soil into place and avoid disturbing the rooting powder on the stem.

Dip stem in rooting hormone powder.

Put hormone-covered stem into pre-made hole in rooting medium.

Press hole closed so that growing medium comes into firm contact with stem.

STEP SEVEN

Water the rooting medium lightly and keep the surface evenly moist at all times. The first few days are the most critical for moisture. Clones have no roots to bring water to leaves. Water arrives from leaves and the cut stem until roots can supply it. Water as needed to keep growing medium evenly moist. Do not let it get soggy, and if it does, remove water at once.

Place a tray containing rooting cubes or small containers of rooting medium into a nursery flat so cubes are easy to handle.

STEP EIGHT

Label each clone when planting. If you are taking complete flats of the same clones at the same time, you will need to label the flat.

STEP NINE

Give clones 18–24 hours of fluorescent light. Place clones four to six inches below single or dual fluorescent tubes. Cool white fluorescents (or a combination of warm and cool white) are excellent for rooting. If clones must be placed under an HID, set them on the perimeter of the garden so they receive less intense light; or shade them with a cloth or screen. Place clones four to six feet (1.2–1.8 m) below a 400–1000-watt metal halide bulb.

STEP TEN

Give clones 95–100 percent humidity the first two days after cutting. These are the most critical days for a clone to get over the shock of being cut. Gradually reduce the humidity to 80–85 percent after the first three to four days. A humidity dome or tent will help keep humidity high. Construct the tent out of plastic bags, rigid plastic, or glass. Make sure to leave openings for air to flow in and out of the dome so little clones can breathe. You may need to mist clones several times a day as an alternative to the humidity tent. Some growers mist once or twice a day when plants are under the humidity dome. Remove any sick, rotting, or dead foliage. Keep leaves up off the rooting medium.

Misting clones with water cools foliage and slows transpiration to help traumatized clones retain moisture unavailable from nonexistent roots. Put clones in a warm place to adjust air temperature.

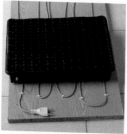

STEP ELEVEN

When the growing medium is a few degrees warmer than the air temperature root growth speeds. A warmer substrate increases underground chemical activity, and lower air temperature slows water loss through leaves. For best results, keep the rooting medium at 75°–80°F (24°–27°C). Growing medium temperatures above 85°F (29°C) may cause root damage. Keep the air temperature 5°–10°F (3°–5.5°C) cooler than the substrate.

Put a heating pad, heating cables, or an incandescent light bulb under the rooting medium to increase root zone temperature.

STEP TWELVE

Ideally none of the clones will wilt or loose rigidity. In the beginning you may have some clones that wilt but become rigid in a few days. Clones that are still wilted after seven days will grow slowly or develop a problem. Set them aside and let them root longer. If they continue to root slowly or show signs of rot at the soil line, toss them out.

STEP THIRTEEN

The new root system will sprout from the buried stem in one to three weeks. In 10–21 days you should see roots growing out the sides of the rooting cubes. Signals that roots have started to grow include yellow leaf tips, roots growing out drain holes, and vertical growth of the clones. To check for root growth in flats or pots, carefully remove the root ball and clone from the pot to see if it has good root development.

Clones usually look strong and healthy soon after you take them. After five or six days, leaves may start to change color. Leaves stay small and often turn a deeper shade of green. After about a week, lower leaves may start to yellow if their nutrient levels dissipate. These clones are using all their resources to conserve moisture and grow new roots. Some dieback in lower leaves is not a sign the plant is dying.

Any sign of slime, pests, or disease means there are problems, and clones should be removed from the garden.

STEP FOURTEEN

Transplant only the strongest well-rooted clones with a dense root system growing out the sides and bottom of rooting cubes. Do not transplant slow-rooting clones or clones with a small root system. Keep slow-growing clones rooting until adequate roots have developed. Do not move clones below bright light until they have fully developed root systems. Once transplanted, clones are ready to harden-off and move into the grow room or to an outdoor garden.
(See Transplanting on the following page).

Set up a vegetative pre-growing area that is lit with an HID or bright compact fluorescent lamp (CFL) for the rooted clones. Place them in this area to let them grow during the first week or two of vegetation. This area needs to be just big enough to accommodate plants from the time they are a few inches tall until they are about a foot tall and ready to be moved into the flowering room.

Transplanting

Transplant clones before they are too big for their containers so they can continue rapid growth. Restrained cramped root systems grow sickly, stunted, rootbound plants. Signs of rootbound plants include slow, weak growth and branches that develop with more distance between limbs. Severely rootbound plants tend to grow straight up with few branches that stretch beyond the sides of the pot.

To check for a restricted root zone, carefully remove the root ball from its pot to see if roots are deeply matted on the bottom or ringing the container. A somewhat dry root ball is usually easy to remove from the pot. The more rootbound the plant, the easier it is to remove. Plants must be sufficiently rooted to withstand being yanked out of the pot!

When growing short plants that reach full maturity in 90 days, there is little need for containers larger than three gallons (11 L). A large mother plant will need a large pot if it will be kept for more than a few months.

Water the clones until water freely flows from the drain holes. Next, fill containers full of growing medium and saturate with water.

Carefully turn each container upside down and tenderly shake the intact root ball into your hand.

Carefully place the root ball into a pre-made hole in the growing medium inside the larger container.

Gingerly pack more potting soil around the wet root ball and water the transplanted seedlings heavily with a fertilizer solution containing vitamin B_1 which will ease transplant shock.

6 Add a little more growing medium if necessary. Use a screen to diffuse light if plants are in a small room. It will take them one to four days to recover from transplant shock. Start fertilizing with a mild fertilizer mix two or three days after transplanting. Keep the soil moist but not soggy. If transplanting rockwool cubes into soil, do not let the cube stay too wet or roots will not grow into soil. Keep the humidity around 70–80 percent and the little ladies should perk right up and show signs of growth in a few days.

Once the first clone is transplanted and watered, move to the next clone and repeat the process. After you get good at each step, you complete tasks in batches. Move the transplants to the perimeter of the HID garden for a day or two until they recover and show signs of growth.

CHAPTER 8

Harvesting

INTRODUCTION

Harvest when plants are at peak ripeness. Harvest timing is critical. The peak harvest window is open for roughly 5–7 days. Most growers manicure harvested buds before drying them slowly and evenly so THC is preserved. After drying, buds must cure so that full aroma and flavor develop. Like a fine wine, aging (curing) improves taste and fragrance. Once cured, proper storage will ensure buds retain all of their essential qualities.

Before Harvest

Pungent marijuana odors are often a problem around harvesttime. To minimize odors keep the drying and trimming room well ventilated so fragrances do not linger. Keep rooms cool, below 70°F (21°C) so essential cannabis oils release few pungent aromas. An air conditioner works well to keep odors to a minimum in sealed rooms. A carbon filter will remove odors in the drying/manicuring room and will also treat expelled air.

Irrigate with plain water or clearing solution to remove residual fertilizers in foliage and soil. Give plants plain water the last 7–14 days before harvest. Make sure to let 10–20 percent of the water drain out the bottom of containers. Clearing solutions remove fertilizer residue faster and are used the last few days before harvest.

77

How to tell when fertilizer will affect taste

- Leaf tips and fringes are burned
- Leaves are brittle at harvest
- Buds crackle when burning
- Buds smell like chemicals
- Buds taste like fertilizer

Change the nutrient solution to plain water in recirculating hydroponic systems 7–10 days before harvest. Continue to top off the reservoir with "fresh" water until harvest, or use a clearing solution as per directions.

Do not water for 1–2 days before harvest, so plants are pre-dried at harvest. Let the soil dry out but do not let the plants wilt.

Give plants total darkness for 48 hours just before harvest so that more resin develops on buds.

Harvest

At harvest all plant growth and THC production stop. THC content *cannot* increase after harvest. In fact, it can only decline. Slow THC decomposition by keeping harvested buds out of extended exposure to light and warm temperatures (above 75°F [24°C]); jostling and bruising from handling; and damp, humid environments.

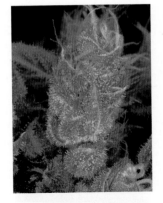

Mind-bending psychoactive THC (tetrahydrocannibinol) is located in leaves, flower buds, and stalked glandular trichomes. The majority of THC is found on female (sinsemilla) plants in the resin glands or trichomes on flower tops. Stalked trichomes look like a small post with a ball on top. These trichomes develop most heavily on buds and small leaves. THC is most concentrated where the stalk meets the ball of the resin gland.

Large female leaves like the Yumboldt at right and male plants contain fewer resin glands and much less mind-altering THC. The THC content found in stems and roots is virtually nonexistent. Male plants, stems, and large leaves hold low levels of THC and are most efficiently used to make hash, concentrated resin.

Harvesting Leaves

Remove large leaves while plants are still in the ground. Cut or pluck off the entire leaf and leaf stem. Once the large leaves are fully formed, THC potency has generally peaked. Smaller leaves around buds continue to develop resin until buds are ripe. Peak potency is retained as long as leaves are healthy and green. Harvest yellow and diseased leaves and dispose of them.

Toss leaves into a paper bag, not a plastic bag. Paper bags breathe well and can be closed by folding over the top.

Keep the paper bag in a closet or area with 45–55 percent humidity and 65°–75°F (18°–24°C) temperature. Reach into the bag once or twice a day and turn leaves so the moist leaves mix with drier leaves. Leaves will be dry to the touch in 5–7 days. Once dry, place leaves in the freezer so they are ready to make hash.

Male Harvest

Harvest male plants before they disperse pollen. Most growers remove them from the garden as soon as they are spotted at pre-flowering, near the end of vegetative growth. Male flowers produce visible pollen sacks with viable pollen 2–4 weeks after lights are set to a 12-hour day/night photoperiod.

Put a plastic bag over any male plants that might disperse pollen before cutting the main trunk off at the base. Shake the plant as little as possible to minimize any pollen dissemination. See *Marijuana Horticulture: The Indoor/Outdoor Medical Grower's Bible* for complete information on breeding.

Male plant in early flowering. The white spots are drops of water.

Sinsemilla Harvest

Harvest sinsemilla plants 6–12 weeks after inducing flowering with the 12/12 day/night photoperiod. Harvest at the point when THC production is at its peak, before it starts to degrade. Most plants that receive the same amount of light throughout are ready to harvest at the same time. Lower buds that receive less light often take a few more days to mature.

In general, *indica* and *indica*-dominant strains are ripe 6–8 weeks after initiating flowering. *Sativa* and *sativa*-dominant strains are ready to harvest in 8–12 weeks. Too often growers harvest too early because they are excited to have a crop.

A plastic bag helps contain male pollen.

sativa-dominant

indica-dominant

Test for ripeness by removing a small piece of a mature bud. Put it in a microwave oven or conventional oven. Set the microwave on a low power setting and turn on in 10-second bursts until it is dry enough to burn. Place a little bit of the dry bud in a single-hit pipe and sample. The dry, raspy taste will be from fast drying, but you will be able to tell how potent the pot is.

Too Early!

This bud is weeks from harvest. Wait at least 6 weeks before testing buds for harvest. Many growers harvest lightweight buds before THC develops to full potential.

Early Harvest

This bud is still a couple weeks from harvest. The healthy, white fuzzy pistils are still growing and the resin is really starting to accumulate. After a couple of weeks, this bud will be packed with resin. Buds harvested now will yield up to 30 percent less weight.

If harvested a little *early* pure *sativa* and *sativa*-dominant plants contain lower concentrations of all cannabinoids; the stone is often more heady and soaring. Pure *indica* and *indica*-dominant strains tend to yield a somewhat less intense body stone.

Peak Harvest

Resin gland formation slows. Trichomes are starting to degrade faster than they develop. THC production has peaked out. Now is the best time to harvest.

Harvest when THC levels are at their *peak* for maximum mind-bending effects. This close up of trichomes shows you what to look for at the time of peak maturity.

Late Harvest

Trichomes start to degrade faster and faster. Harvest now for a heavier high.

White pistils turn brownish-red as buds continue to ripen. In some strains, peak potency is when half of the pistils are white and the other half have turned brown. This test is only a general guide to peak potency.

Harvest *after peak* maturity for higher levels of CBD in relation to THC to yield more of a body stone. *Indica, afghani, indica*-dominant and *afghani*-dominant strains harvested now produce a heavier body couch-lock stone. *Sativa* and *sativa*-dominant strains harvested after peak potency yield more of a body stone too.

The most accurate way to tell peak potency is to look at resin glands on growing plants with a 10X–50X magnifier. My favorite is a 30X handheld microscope with a battery-powered light. You can quickly check several buds daily for peak potency.

Look at the capitate stalked tri-chomes, the ones with a ball on top of the stalk. They develop clear to translucent resinous trichomes. More and more well-formed trichomes continue to appear as they reach peak potency. Harvest when these resin glands form more slowly than they degrade. Bulbous tops and stalks start to deform when they degrade. Handling buds will bruise and deform resin glands. Such damaged resin glands should not be confused with naturally deteriorating ones.

Often resin glands on strains change colors and deteriorate as plants ripen. The trichomes turn from clear to translucent to amber. All glands do not change color at the same time.

Hairlike cystolith trichomes contain no THC. They are visible with the naked eye and with magnification. Find these protective trichomes on tops and bottoms of leaves, stems, and buds. They exude substances that repel pests and protect foliage from diseases.

Step-by-Step: Harvest

STEP ONE

Stop fertilization 10–14 days before harvest. This will allow plants to use built-up nutrients in foliage. Accumulated nutrients in plants cause buds to taste like fertilizer when burned. If you use a "clearing solution" you can fertilize up until the last 3 days before harvest.

STEP TWO

Do not spray plants during harvest week so there are no unwanted residues on foliage at harvest. Sprays can also linger in dense buds, which may attract bud mold.

STEP THREE

Give plants 24–48 hours of *total* darkness before harvest. Growers who do this say the buds are a little more resinous afterward.

STEP FOUR

Cut or pluck off large leaves and leaf stems a day or two before harvest. This will speed the rest of the harvest process, and it does not diminish harvest.

STEP FIVE

Use pruners to cut plants at the base or remove one branch at a time. Cut branches into lengths of 6–24 inches. Do not remove the root ball, it contains absolutely no THC.

STEP SIX

Manicure buds right after harvesting. Trim off smaller leaves around buds that show little resin. Use small, pointed scissors to get into tight spaces in buds. See Manicuring later in this chapter.

STEP SEVEN

Save all trimmed leaves in a paper bag so they can be made into hash later.

STEP EIGHT

Hang manicured branches from drying lines or place on drying racks. Keep the temperature at 65°–75°F (18°–24°C) with the humidity at 45–55 percent.

STEP NINE

Feel buds to check for dryness. They should be dry enough to cure in four to seven days. See Drying, page 89 for more details.

STEP TEN

Once buds appear to be dry, they are ready for the final drying or curing. See Curing, page 91.

After harvest the crop must be manicured, dried and cured.

Manicuring

Manicuring buds is time-consuming. Budget 4–6 hours to manicure a single pound (454 gm) by hand with scissors. An automatic trimmer will cut manicuring time to 1–2 hours.

Use small easy-to-maneuver pointed scissors to reach into crevices in buds. Have 2 or 3 different pairs of scissors available. Switch scissors when your hands fatigue.

Manicure over a fine silkscreen, glass, or slick-surfaced table. Scrape up fallen resin glands on the table or under the screen. This potent resin can be smoked immediately or pressed into blocks of hash.

Wear inexpensive rubber gloves to collect "finger hash." After trimming, remove accumulated finger hash on gloves with rubbing alcohol. Set the hash-laden alcohol on the counter overnight to evaporate. Scrape up the remaining hash after all the alcohol has evaporated. Or put the rubber gloves in a freezer for a few hours. Cooling will make it easier to scrape and rub the accumulated hash from the gloves.

Scrape accumulated resin from scissors when it clogs blades. Use a small knife to remove built-up resin from blades. Ball up small bits of scraped resin by rubbing it together between fingers. The ball of hash will grow as manicuring progresses.

Drying

Fresh green marijuana is not very potent. Drying converts THC into its psychoactive form and removes about 75 percent of the moisture from freshly harvested plants. Moisture evaporates evenly when plants are dried slowly over 5–7 days or longer. Buds are dry throughout so will taste sweet and smoke smooth. Buds dried too quickly retain chlorophyll and other substances within foliage. Such poorly dried cannabis tastes "green," burns unevenly, and tastes bad.

The temperature in the ideal drying room is between 65° and 75°F (18°–24°C) and humidity from 45–55 percent. Temperatures below 65°F (18°C) slow drying, and humidity is more difficult to control. Humidity above 80 percent slows drying and increases the chances of mold attacks. Temperatures above 75°F (24°C) may cause buds to dry too fast, and humidity can also fall below the ideal 50 percent level more easily. Always use an accurate maximum/minimum thermometer and hygrometer to ensure temperature and humidity are kept in the ideal range.

Use a small circulation fan to keep air moving in the drying room, but do not train the fan directly on buds or they will dry unevenly. A ventilation fan may also be necessary to help control temperature and humidity. Use an air conditioner or heater to control extreme humidity and temperatures.

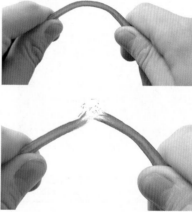

Small harvests can be dried easily in a closet, cabinet, or a cardboard box that is a fraction of the growing area's size. Large harvests require much more room. See *Marijuana Horticulture: The Indoor/Outdoor Medical Grower's Bible* for more information.

Check for dryness by bending a stem. The stem should snap rather than fold when bent. The bud should be dry to touch, but not brittle. Dry buds burn well when rolled into a joint. Once dry, buds are ready to cure. Curing is essential!

Curing and Storage

Once buds are dry, they are ready for curing. The curing process lets buds dry evenly so they smoke smooth and taste sweet. When properly cured, all unnecessary moisture is removed and THC reaches its most psychoactive potential. Proper curing ensures buds are completely dry and much less susceptible to mold when stored.

To cure buds, gently pack them into sealable airtight containers. Moisture will move from stems to drier foliage. Place the containers in a cool, dry, dark place. Open the container after 2–4 hours to let humid air escape. Leave the top off for 5–10 minutes so moisture evacuates. Close the container. Open the container for a few minutes every few hours to release excess moisture before closing the lid again. Depending upon moisture content, buds should be totally dry in a few days to 2 weeks. Gently squeeze buds to feel if they are less pliable and moist than they were a few hours before. Once they are evenly dry, they are ready to smoke or seal in an airtight container for storage.

Store packaged buds in a cool, dry, dark place. The owner of this Volkswagen Beetle stored buds in a cool, dry place, but he forgot to keep it dark. Buds stored in the refrigerator will stay fresh a few months longer. Make sure buds are in an airtight container when stored in the refrigerator to prevent moisture from entering the container.

CHAPTER 9

Grow Gear

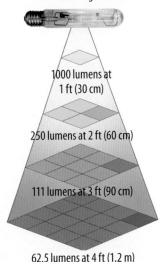

1000-lumen light source

1000 lumens at
1 ft (30 cm)

250 lumens at 2 ft (60 cm)

111 lumens at 3 ft (90 cm)

62.5 lumens at 4 ft (1.2 m)

Lumens decrease as the distance
from the light source increases.

INTRODUCTION

Growing indoors requires grow gear to supply and control light, air, water, and the growing medium. Below is a simple discussion that will give you a basic understanding of the grow gear you will need—what it is and how it works.

Light and Lamps

You will need a light to illuminate your beautiful plants. If you decide to grow in a small space such as a closet or grow cabinet, you can use fluorescent, compact fluorescent (CFL) or HID lights. Fluorescent lamps work well to grow clones, seedlings and small vegetative crops. CFLs can be used to cultivate clones, mothers, and vegetative plants. When CFLs are placed close enough to flowering plants, big tight buds will develop. HID lamps are favored for growing vegetative and flowering plants.

Brilliance: Light fades exponentially fast (see charts). Smaller wattage bulbs can be placed closer to plants. Wattages below 400 are not as efficient converting electricity to light as larger wattage lamps. I prefer 400-watt and 600-watt HID lamps because they are most efficient and can be placed closer to plants. My studies (see *Marijuana Horticulture: The Indoor/Outdoor Medical Grower's Bible*) proved that a 600-watt HP sodium lamp can deliver as much light to a garden as a 1000-watt lamp when using the same reflectors! Using a 600-watt lamp lowers electricity bills and decreases heat in the grow space.

LPW: Lumens per watt is the measure of the conversion from electricity to light energy. Divide watts by lumens to get LPW. The brightest bulbs have a high LPW rating.

175 watts	400 watts	1000 watts
1200–2000	3500–5500	9000–12000
500–1000	1400–3000	5500–8000
250–400	600–1200	2500–4000
	300–500	1500–2000
		500–1200

Wattage and distance lumen comparison (1-foot [30-cm] increments)

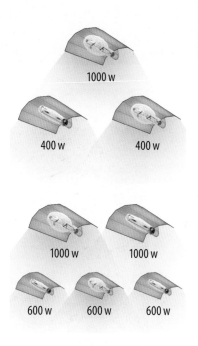

1000 w

400 w   400 w

1000 w   1000 w

600 w   600 w   600 w

Two 400-watt HID lamps illuminate plants better than a single 1000-watt lamp because they emit light from two different points. These points (bulbs) can be placed closer to plants. A single 1000-watt lamp must be placed 24–36 inches (60–90 cm) above plants. A 400-watt lamp can be placed from 12–24 inches (30–60 cm) above the garden. Each foot closer nearly doubles light intensity.

Use fluorescent, CFL, metal halide, or HP sodium bulbs to grow cannabis. Other bulbs—incandescent, tungsten halogen, LP sodium, mercury vapor—have poor spectrums and are not efficient enough to grow cannabis.

Spectrum: The color spectrum of lamps is measured in kelvin (K). Cannabis grows within a spectrum of 2000 K and 6000 K.

PAR watts: Photosynthetically active radiation measures the specific amount of photons (a measure of light energy) a plant needs to grow. The higher the PAR rating of a bulb, the more efficient it is for growing cannabis.

Fluorescent tubes grow great clones and seedlings.

Fluorescent Tubes

Grow clones, seedlings, and vegetative plants with fluorescents. Flowering plants develop smaller, less-dense buds under fluorescents.

Wattages available: 15–44, in lengths from 18–48 inches (50–100 cm)

Brilliance: Fluorescent lamps range from bright to brighter. Their long shape and low lumen output make it necessary to keep tubes 1–2 inches above plants. Brighter T5 and T8 bulbs can be 4–6 inches above plants. New thin bulbs are brighter than larger tubes. Fluorescent bulbs are classified by the diameter of the tube. See table below.

BULB	DIAMETER	LPW
T12	1.5 inch (5 cm)	68
T8	1 inch (3 cm)	100
T5	0.625 inch (1.5 cm)	92

Spectrum: Thermodynamic temperature is measured in kelvin (K). The popular color spectrums are from 3000 K (warm white), 4200 K (cool white), to 5000 K (daylight/natural sunlight). Use a combination of warm and cool white bulbs, or one with a spectrum of about 5000 K.

Life of bulb: Rated at 20,000–30,000 hours. Most growers replace bulbs after 2 years of operation at 24 hours a day. Take lamp and ballast to a specialty recycling center for electronic devices.

Fluorescent tubes can be set up to illuminate vegetative plants with outstanding results.

A fluorescent lamp requires a *ballast*. The T12 fixtures use analog and digital ballasts. The T8 and the T5 fixtures use electronic ballasts that run cooler and cycle electricity faster so lights do not flicker.

CFL (Compact Fluorescent Lamps)

Grow clones, seedlings, and vegetative plants with CFLs. Keep CFLs close to flowering plants so they develop big, tight buds.

Wattages available: 26–200, in lengths from 6–20 inches (15–50 cm)

Brilliance: CFLs produce very bright light with relatively low wattage. The best values are 55–65-watt bulbs (see CFL Watt and Lumen Chart on the next page). These bulbs are bright and inexpensive. Smaller wattages are less bright and very low wattage. Larger wattages are bright but more expensive.

Keep CFL lamps close to plants.

Stems stretch in low light.

Long U-shaped CFL lamps distribute light evenly over their entire length.

Spectrum: The color spectrum is delivered at 2700 K (warm white) to 5000 K (cool white) in a selection of bulbs. Warm white CFLs (2700 K) have more red in the spectrum and can be used alone but are best used in conjunction with cool white lamps to avoid internodal stretching during flowering.

Life of bulb: Rated at 8000–15,000 hours. Most growers replace bulbs after 1 to 1.5 years of operation at 18 hours per day. Take lamp and ballast to a specialty recycling center for electronic devices.

WATTS	SPACE COVERED	DISTANCE ABOVE PLANTS
55–65	12 × 12 in (30 × 30 cm)	1–2 in (4–6 cm)
80–120	24 × 24 in (60 × 60 cm)	2–3 in (6–9 cm)
150–200	30 × 30 in (75 × 75 cm)	3–4 in (9–12 cm)

CFL WATT AND LUMEN CHART	
WATTS	INITIAL LUMENS
26	1800
55	3500
60	4000
65	4500
85	6000
95	7600
120	9000
125	9500
150	12,000
200	15,000

A ballast is required by a CFL. New electronic ballasts make CFL lamps run coolly and efficiently. Remote electronic ballasts stay with the fixture after the bulb burns out. Attached ballasts are recycled with the bulb.

Energy-saving spiral-shaped CFLs work well to grow clones and seedlings.

Short U-shaped CFL offers the best value in 55–65 watt size.

LED Lamps

LED (light-emitting diode) lamps could be the future of indoor plant lighting. These inherently efficient lamps use solid state lighting to illuminate, rather than filaments used by incandescent and tungsten halogen bulbs, or gas which is used in HID, fluorescent, and compact fluorescent bulbs. LED lamps consume a fraction of the electricity of HID and fluorescent/CFL lamps and generate very little heat. LED fixtures are rated for regular household current—120 V and 240 V.

Grow clones, seedlings, and vegetative plants with LED lamps. Flowering plants develop smaller, less-dense buds under LEDs.

LED light output continues to increase with improved materials and technological advances while maintaining efficiency and reliability associated with solid state equipment. Do not be fooled by old LED lamps that are not as bright as new models. *Do not purchase LED lamps with a rating lower than 1 (one) watt per bulb.*

Wattages available: LED lamps are rated in milliwatts (mW) and consume much less electricity than fluorescent, CFL, and HID lamps to generate much more light. Currently the most common LEDs used for plant growth consume 1 watt per bulb. Typically clusters of 80–100 bulbs consuming 80–100 watts respectively are placed in a single fixture.

WATTS	SPACE COVERED	DISTANCE ABOVE PLANTS
85–90	36 × 36 in (60 × 60 cm)	12–24 in (30–60 cm)

Brilliance: Directional LEDs ensure that all the light produced is pointed downward so that no light fragments off to the side. LEDs from Philips Lumileds Lighting Company produce 115 lumens per watt.

NOTE: The exact spectrum produced is such efficient light to grow plants that previous rules of thumb about lumens-per-watt do not apply. For example, an 85–90-watt LED fixture with the proper spectrum will illuminate a 3 × 3-foot grow room.

Spectrum: The color spectrum of each bulb is dictated by the semiconducting material composition and condition. The spectrum can range from infrared to ultraviolet and many colors in between. The new LED "grow" lamps combine blue and red bulbs to form the exact spectrum necessary for cannabis growth.

Life of fixture: LED fixtures have a 100-percent-efficient life expectancy of 30,000 hours—about 6 years when operated 12 hours a day, and 3 years when operated 24 hours a day. Beyond 30,000 hours, brilliance fades approximately 30 percent during the following 20,000 hours.

Ballast: Similar to a ballast the power supply that drives LEDs precisely regulates the flow of electricity in milliwatts to the lamps. The solid state low-wattage device generates very little heat because the flow is not impaired. Several fixtures available today include a fan(s) to dissipate heat quickly and efficiently.

HID Lamps

Use high intensity discharge (HID) lamps to grow vegetative and flowering marijuana indoors. The two most common HID lamps are metal halide, which have a clear or "white" light spectrum, and high pressure (HP) sodium (right), which have a yellowish-orange spectrum.

Cannabis can grow from seedling to harvest under a metal halide lamp. You can also add or switch to an HP sodium for flowering. Add another lamp during flowering to increase light intensity and fatten up buds.

HP sodium lamps produce yellowish light.

Metal halide light is white.

High intensity discharge (HID) lamps that work well to grow marijuana are available in the following wattages, and cover the following amount of floor space.

NOTE: the figures to the right assume lamps are covered with an efficient reflective hood.

WATTS	SPACE COVERED	DISTANCE ABOVE PLANTS
150	2 × 2 ft (60 × 60 cm)	12 in (30 cm)
175	2 × 2 ft (60 × 60 cm)	12 in (30 cm)
250	2.5 × 2.5 ft (75 × 75 cm)	14 in (40 cm)
400	3 × 3 ft (90 × 90 cm)	18 in (45 cm)
600	3.5 × 3.5 ft (105 × 105 cm)	20–24 in (50–60 cm)
1000	4 × 4 ft (1.2 × 1.2 m)	24–36 in (60–90 cm)
1100	4 × 4 ft (1.2 × 1.2 m)	24–36 in (60–90 cm)

(The 1100-watt bulbs are not a good value.)

capacitor   transformer   mogul socket

A ballast is required for a metal halide or HP sodium HID lamp. Conventional analog ballasts contain a transformer, capacitor, and connecting wiring. Some HP sodium ballasts have a starter. The transformer and capacitor can be attached to the mogul light socket or connected by an electrical cord to a remote ballast. Attached ballasts are connected to the mogul socket and bulb. The ballast generates heat and should be placed outside of grow room. Do not attach ballasts to extension cords, or the voltage will drop and light will dim.

Unlike conventional ballasts, electronic ballasts are lightweight, use less electricity, and produce little or no electricity-wasting heat. Most electronic ballasts can be used with either 120 or 220 volts, either 50 or 60 cycles, and either metal halide or HP sodium lamps. However, they have a relatively high failure rate of about 10 percent on 400-watt, 600-watt, and 1000-watt lamps. Failure rates for smaller wattages are much lower.

Disposal: Take lamp and ballast to a specialty recycling center. Do not dump where they will wind up in a landfill.

Metal Halide Lamps

Grow vegetative and flowering plants efficiently with metal halide bulbs.

Wattages available: 150, 175, 250, 400, 600, 1000, 1100

Brilliance: There are many different metal halide bulbs. Super bulbs are always brighter than standards. Bulbs are available in many different models. Some bulbs with the same wattage are brighter than others.

Spectrum: Metal halide bulbs are readily available in a spectrum range of 3000, 4000, and 5500 K.

Life of bulb: Rated at 12,000 hours. Most growers replace bulbs after 12 months of operation. Take lamp and ballast to a specialty recycling center. Do not dump where they will wind up in a landfill.

Metal halide lights in this mother room are supported by CFLs.

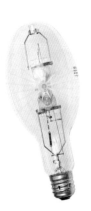

Metal halide lamps grow both vegetative and flowering plants.

HP Sodium Lamps

HP sodium lamps are most often used in flowering rooms, but they can also be used to grow vegetative plants. Stems tend to stretch about 10 percent more when using exclusively HP sodium bulbs.

Wattages available: 150, 175, 250, 400, 600, 1000

Brilliance: HP sodium lamps are more efficient than metal halides at converting electricity to light.

There are many different HP sodium bulbs. Super bulbs are always brighter than standards. Bulbs are available in many different models. Some bulbs with the same wattage are brighter than other models.

Spectrum: The color spectrum of the bulb is limited to the reddish-yellow end of the spectrum. HP sodium bulbs are readily available in a spectrum range of 2100 K to 2200 K.

Life of bulb: Rated at 24,000 hours. Most growers replace bulbs after 18–24 months of operation.

A 430-watt Son Agro bulb with more blue in the spectrum is more effective at keeping plants from stretching than if a standard HP sodium were used.

A 600-watt HP sodium lamp is the most efficient HID available.

Conversion Lamps

Most efficiently used to grow vegetative and flowering plants.

Wattages available: 150, 215, 360, 400, 880, 940, 1000

Brilliance: There are two basic types of conversion, or retrofit, bulbs: 1. To use a metal halide system with a bulb that emits light similar to an HP sodium bulb. 2. Retrofit HP sodium to convert it into a virtual metal halide system. Conversion bulbs operate at a lower wattage and are not as bright as HP sodium bulbs. Although conversion bulbs have less blue, they are up to 25 percent brighter than metal halide systems and their LPW conversion is better than that of super metal halides.

Spectrum: Conversion bulbs have a similar kelvin temperature to that of their metal halide and HP sodium counterparts.

Life of bulb: Rated at 24,000 hours. Most growers replace bulbs after 18–24 months of operation. Take lamp and ballast to a specialty recycling center for electronic devices.

Reflective Hoods

Use an efficient horizontal reflective hood to direct the most light from a bulb toward plants. A good reflective hood provides 10–40 percent more light than an inefficient one. The ideal reflector can be placed close to the garden canopy and will distribute light evenly.

A reflective hood that distributes light evenly—with no bright hot spots—can be placed closer to plants without burning them. When the lamp is closer, the light plants receive is more intense. In addition to reflective walls, the proper reflective hood over the lamp can double the growing area.

Reflective hoods are made from steel sheet metal, aluminum, or even stainless steel. Some hood manufacturers apply (Titanium) white paint in a powder-coating process. The pebble and hammer-tone surfaces offer good light diffusion and more surface area to reflect light. Hot spots are commonplace among highly polished, mirrorlike surfaces. Mirror-polished hoods also scratch easily and create uneven lighting.

Horizontal reflective hoods tend to have a hot spot directly under the bulb. To dissipate this hot spot of light and lower the heat it creates, some manufacturers install a light deflector below the bulb. The deflector diffuses the light and heat directly under the bulb. When there is no hot spot, reflective hoods with deflectors can be placed closer to plants.

Horizontal reflectors direct half of the light downward toward plants, requiring only half of the light to be reflected. Selecting an efficient reflective hood will increase the efficiency of your lamp.

Lightweight reflective hoods with open ends or sides dissipate heat quickly. Extra air flows directly through the hood and around the bulb in open-ended fixtures to cool the bulb and the fixture. Aluminum dissipates heat more quickly than steel. Train a fan on reflective hoods to speed heat loss.

Vertical reflective hoods with vertical lamps are less efficient than horizontal ones. Reflected light travels farther before being reflected in parabolic or cone-shaped reflective hoods.

The closer you put the reflector to the bulb, the more intense the light it reflects. Enclosed hoods with a glass shield covering the bulb operate at higher temperatures. The glass shield is a barrier between plants and the hot bulb. Enclosed hoods must have enough vents; otherwise, heat buildup in the fixture causes bulbs to burn out prematurely. Water-cooled and air-cooled lamp fixtures are somewhat popular in hot climates. These lamps run cooler and can be moved closer to plants.

Using no reflective hood is an option. With no reflector, the lamp burns cooler and emits only direct light. The lamps must be suspended between plants to be used most efficiently.

Reflective Walls

Reflective walls increase the light that plants on the perimeter of the garden receive by up to 10 percent. Paint walls white or hang white plastic Visqueen or reflective Mylar to increase light reflection on the garden's perimeter. Keep plants within a few inches of reflective walls to maximize reflective efficiency.

More Light

Plants that have just entered the flowering room can stay on the perimeter of the garden for a month until the more mature plants directly under lamp have finished flowering. This simple trick can easily increase harvests by 5–10 percent.

A light mover moves lamps back and forth or in circles across the ceiling of a grow room. The linear or circular path distributes light evenly. Use a light mover to get lights closer to plants. Keep plants at least 12 inches away from a lamp on a light mover. The closer a lamp is to plants without burning them, the more light plants receive.

Manually rotate plants so light reaches all the foliage to promote more even development. Use a light mover or put the containers on wheels to make the job easier.

Add a shallow shelf around the perimeter of the garden to use light that is shunted into walls. Use brackets to put up a 4 to 6-inch-wide (10–15 cm) shelf around the perimeter. The shelf can be built on a slight angle and lined with plastic to form a runoff canal.

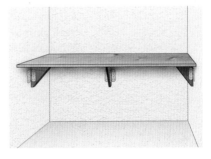

Air

Ventilation, Circulation, Temperature, Humidity, CO₂, Fragrance

Fresh air is necessary in all indoor gardens. It is easy to obtain and inexpensive to maintain. Air ventilation often makes the difference between a heavy harvest and crop failure. Fresh air brings carbon dioxide (CO_2) necessary for plant life into the room. A good ventilation system expels CO_2-poor air. Air ventilation is also essential to keep temperature and humidity at proper levels for fast plant growth. Both intake and exit vents are essential for adequate airflow in and out of the grow space. A circulation fan is also necessary to keep the air from stratifying into hot and cold layers inside the room.

Air Ventilation

Install air exit vents in the hottest part of the room—usually the highest point—for passive, silent air venting. The larger the diameter of the exhaust ducts, the more air that moves out. Airflow is usually inadequate with just an air vent. Add an exhaust fan to make the air move faster out the air vent and increase airflow in the room.

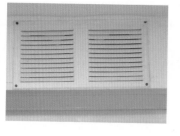

A fresh-air intake vent is necessary to create a flow of fresh air into the room. The vent can be in the form of cracks in the grow room walls, a space under the door, or an actual louvered vent. It must allow enough air to enter the grow room so there is an adequate flow of fresh air into the room.

Locate intake vent(s) near the floor so they bring in cooler air. An exhaust fan vented outdoors that pulls new air through the vent usually creates a sufficient flow of air. If passive airflow through the vent is inadequate, attach a fan to draw air *into* the room.

A slight vacuum inside the room that keeps the door closed generally provides the perfect scenario. The ratio of 1:4 (100 cfm [170 m³/h] incoming and 400 cfm [680 m³/h] outgoing) will give the room a little negative pressure and keep the door closed.

Fresh air entering the room should be about the same temperature as air within the room so that plants do not suffer temperature stress. Cover the intake vent with fine mesh silkscreen to help exclude pests.

Ratio = 1:4 – four times more air exits than enters the room

Squirrel cage fan

Grow spaces must have an exhaust vent or an extraction fan. The air must change in the room every 1–5 minutes. Air in small grow spaces should change every minute. A vent fan *pulls* air out of a room 4 times more efficiently than a fan is able to *push* it out.

Axial fans are quiet and move air efficiently when properly installed. Attach the fan to a rheostat (fader switch) to control the speed, or to a thermostat. Turn fans down to the point at which they make virtually no noise and will still keep the room a cool 75°F (24°C) during the day and 70°F (21°C) at night.

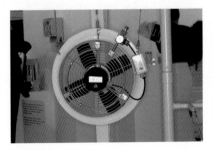

Exhaust or extraction fans are rated in cubic feet per minute (cfm) or cubic meters per hour (m^3/h) of air volume they can move. The fan should be able to replace the air volume (length × width × height = total volume) of the grow room in 1–5 minutes.

ROOM SIZE	FAN CFM (M^3/H)
2 × 2 ft (60 × 90 cm)	40 (68)
3 × 3 ft (90 × 90 cm)	60 (102)
4 × 4 ft (1.2 × 1.2 m)	100 (170)
5 × 5 ft (1.5 × 1.5 m)	150 (255)
6 × 6 ft (1.8 × 1.8 m)	250 (425)
7 × 7 ft (2.1 × 2.1 m)	400 (680)
8 × 8 ft (2.4 × 2.4 m)	500 (850)

Propeller or muffin fans with large fan blades expel air through a large opening and are most efficient and quiet when balanced, well oiled, and operated at low RPM.

Inline fans are designed to fit into ducting. The propellers are mounted to increase the airflow quickly, effortlessly, and as quietly as possible. Inline fans are available in quiet, high-quality models that run smoothly.

High-speed computer fans are efficient for their small size and create little noise.

Air Circulation

An oscillating circulation fan is essential in all grow rooms. Mount circulation fans on walls or the ceiling of the grow room. Mount at least one 12–16-inch (30–40 cm) oscillating fan for every 400–600 watts of light. Mount the fan(s) far enough away from plants so that the turbulent air makes leaves flutter a little. Make sure circulation fan is not set in a fixed position and blowing too hard on tender plants. It could cause windburn and dry out plants, especially small seedlings and clones. Remove the outer shroud of fans with plastic propellers to reduce resistance on the motor. This will extend the life of the motor and prevent fires!

Foliage is packed in tightly during flowering; extra air circulation helps keep bud mold from forming during the last two weeks before harvest. Trim plants from the bottom up to allow more air to circulate between plants.

Oscillating fans that are affixed to the wall or ceiling work well to circulate air in small grow spaces. They are easy to move and direct air where needed.

Felt or rubber grommets below each foot of the fan will reduce noise caused by vibrations.

Air Ducting

Vent fans are usually attached to ducting to direct air out of the grow room. Flexible ducting is easier to use than rigid ducting. Keep the ducting straight and short. Long runs of ducting cause less air to be expelled and at a slower rate. When ducting turns more than 30 degrees, air movement declines and less air exits the other end.

Ducting at **no angle** moves the **most** air.

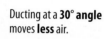

Ducting at a **30° angle** moves **less** air.

Ducting at a **45° angle** moves **less** air.

Ducting at a **90° angle** moves the **least** air.

Direct used grow room air out a chimney, roof vent, or window so that it does not bother neighbors with the telltale smell of a lush marijuana garden.

See Fragrance on page 116 for more information on ducting.

Air Temperature and Humidity

Use the vent fan, heater, and air conditioner to maintain the proper temperature and humidity in the grow room. If the grow room contains a heat and air conditioning vent, use it to supply extra heat or cold air, and to aid air circulation.

Keep the temperature about 75°F (24°C) during the day and 60°–70°F (16°–21°C) at night in both vegetative and flowering rooms. This is a basic guideline. A couple of degrees warmer is OK.

Keep the humidity about 60 percent day and night in the vegetative room.

Keep the humidity about 50 percent day and night in the flowering room.

Install a thermostat and/or a humidistat and attach to the vent fan to automatically turn the vent fan on and off to help control temperature.

Install a maximum/minimum thermometer and hygrometer in all grow rooms. For the most accurate temperature readings install a thermometer near the ceiling, another at the canopy level of plants, and another near the floor. Take temperature readings before lights go on, once in the heat of the day, and 30 minutes after lights go out. Record the temperature and humidity each time and make sure to keep them at the proper levels.

Use an inexpensive rheostat to regulate the speed of vent fans and control temperature and humidity.

This standard heat pump/air conditioner thermostat interior shows liquid mercury bubble that is used to regulate temperature.

Automatic controllers available at hydroponics stores make it very easy to manage the grow room atmosphere.

Carbon Dioxide (CO$_2$) Enrichment

Cannabis can use more CO$_2$ than the 0.04 percent (400 ppm) that naturally occurs in the air. By enriching the amount of CO$_2$ to 0.12–0.15 percent (1200–1500 ppm), plants can grow up to 30 percent faster, providing that genetics, light, water, and nutrients are not limiting. CO$_2$ levels above 5000 ppm are not advised for people.

With CO$_2$, plants use nutrients, water, and space at a faster rate. A higher temperature, from 75°–80°F (24°–27°C) will help stimulate more rapid metabolism.

Keeping temperature and humidity at proper levels is the key to growing healthy plants.

CO$_2$ level can be measured with inexpensive disposable tests and more expensive infrared monitoring systems. CO$_2$ levels can also be controlled with an electronic device.

CO_2 Emitter Systems

CO_2 emitter systems produce no toxic gases, heat, or water. They are also precise, metering an exact amount of CO_2 into the room from a cylinder of compressed gas.

Buying a complete CO_2 emitter system at a hydroponics store is usually the best option for small indoor growers.

When full, a 50-pound steel tank weighs 170 pounds (77 kg). A full 20-pound (9 kg) steel tank weighs 70 pounds (32 kg). A full 20-pound (9 kg) aluminum tank weighs about 50 pounds (23 kg), and a full 35-pound (16 kg) tank weights 75 pounds (34 kg). Most suppliers exchange tanks and refill them. The tanks are also safety inspected once a year.

Carbon dioxide is very cold when released, and once in the atmosphere, CO_2 is heavier and cooler than air and cascades onto the plants below. A good air circulation system is essential to keep air mixed.

This compress CO_2 tank has an on/off valve, pressure regulator and a flow meter. The unit emits the precise amount of CO_2 into the room.

CO_2 Generator Systems

CO_2 generator systems that burn natural gas or LP (propane) gas to produce CO_2 are less expensive to operate than emitter systems, but they produce heat and water as byproducts of the combustion process. Generators use a pilot light with a flow meter and burner enclosed in a protective housing.

Operate the generators manually or synchro-nize them with a timer to operate with other grow room equipment such as ventilation fans. CO_2 is heavier and colder than the ambient air, so you must have good air circulation for even distribution of CO_2.

Other Ways to Make CO_2 include compost, fermentation, dry ice, baking soda and vinegar. See *Marijuana Horticulture: The Indoor/Outdoor Medical Marijuana Grower's Bible* for more information.

Fragrance

Cannabis has the most pungent fragrance from when it begins to flower through the end of harvest. Before flowering, many strains of growing marijuana have little fragrance that the exhaust fan can carry outdoors discreetly. A good exhaust fan, vented outdoors, is the first step in cannabis odor control and the easiest way to keep the house from reeking of fresh marijuana. Neutralize odors with masking agents and charcoal filters. Masking agents are most effective at exhaust exits, hallways, and doors. Charcoal filters actually remove unwanted fragrance from the air before it is expelled from the room.

Masking Agents

Essential oils available in several products actually kill odors by creating a neutral atmosphere at the atomic level. Such products are usually available in gel and spray. The deodorizers can be set out in the room, around the house, and near doorways. Other products are designed to be attached to the ventilation ductwork system.

NOTE: New lightweight carbon filters have recently appeared on the market.

Activated Carbon Filters

Activated charcoal filters absorb odor molecules and other pollutants in the air. They require three things to work properly.

1. Humidity must be below 55 percent. Above 65–70 percent relative humidity, the charcoal absorbs so much moisture that it clogs.
2. Air must move slowly through charcoal filters to extract odors
3. Use a pre-filter to remove dust, and change it every 60 days

Do not use activated carbon that is "crushed." It is less efficient than charcoal pellets. For more information and websites that sell carbon filters, check Chapter 10: Grow Cabinets, Closets, and Rooms, Step Seven: Neutralize Odors.

Water

Clean, balanced water is essential to grow marijuana. Water that tastes good to drink is usually okay for plants. Good water typically has the proper pH (acid to alkaline balance) and EC (electrical conductivity that measures dissolved solids). Bad water must be altered before using. Moving this water to irrigate plants also presents a few interesting challenges to indoor growers.

pH

The pH scale, from 0–14, measures acid-to-alkaline balance. Zero is the most acidic, 7 is neutral, and 14 is most alkaline. Every full-point change in pH signifies a tenfold increase or decrease in acidity or alkalinity. For example, soil or water with a pH of 5 is 10 times more acidic than water or soil with a pH of 6.

Different mediums perform best at different pH levels. Follow manufacturer's guidelines for pH level, and correct the pH using the manufacturer's suggested chemicals.

Stabilize the pH of the water before adding fertilizer. Make a correction if readings vary ± one-half point. Deviations in pH levels often affect nutrient solubility.

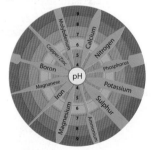

Soil pH

The pH of the nutrient solution controls the availability of (nutrient) ions that cannabis needs to grow. Marijuana grows well hydroponically within a pH range of 5.5–6.5, with 6.0 being ideal for soil and 5.5–6.5 for hydroponics.

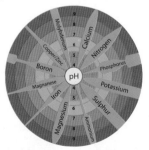

Hydroponic pH

In hydroponics, the nutrients are in solution and more available than when in soil. The pH of the solution can fluctuate a half point and not cause any problems. When the pH is above 7 or below 5.5, some nutrients are not absorbed as quickly as possible. Check the pH every day or two.

Use an electronic pH meter to measure water and nutrient solution pH. You can also measure the pH of soil, soilless substrates, and water and nutrient solutions with an electronic pH pen when the substrate is mixed with water.

Fine dolomite lime, a compound of magnesium (Mg) and calcium (Ca), keeps the soil pH stable. Add 1 cup per cubic foot (25 cl to 30 liters) to keep potting soil pH stable.

Hydrated lime is only calcium and water-soluble. Be very careful when using and do not use more than 0.25 cup per cubic foot (6 cl per 30 liters).

Raise water and nutrient solution pH with calcium carbonate, potassium hydroxide, or sodium hydroxide. Both hydroxides are caustic and require special handling.

Lower water and nutrient solution pH: Phosphoric and nitric acid can be used to lower pH, as can calcium nitrate, but it is less common. Aspirin also lowers the pH. However, hormonal reactions appear to be triggered by aspirin. Some growers report more hermaphrodites when using aspirin to alter the pH.

This grower added fine dolomite lime to the soil before planting and harvested big Blueberry buds!

EC/PPM
EC, TDS, DS, CF, PPM Meters

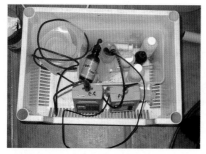

Using an electronic EC (ppm) meter is the most accurate way to measure the strength of the nutrient solution.

Measure the EC (ppm) of the nutrient solution before irrigating.

Fertilizers (nutrients) carry an electrical current when dissolved in water. Nutrient (salt) concentrations are measured by their ability to conduct electricity through a nutrient solution. Add elemental salts/metals to a solution and electrical conductivity increases proportionately. Simple electronic meters measure this value and interpret it as total. Every salt in a multielement solution has a different conductivity factor.

Electrical conductivity (EC), conductivity factor (CF), and parts per million (ppm) are the scales used to measure conductivity. American growers use ppm to measure overall fertilizer concentration. European, Australian, and New Zealand growers use EC. Some still use CF in parts of Australia and New Zealand.

Nutrient solutions used to grow marijuana generally range between 500 and 2000 ppm. A dissolved solids (DS) measurement indicates how many parts per million (ppm) of dissolved solids exist in a solution. A reading of 1800 ppm means there are 1800 parts of nutrient in one million parts solution, or 1800/1,000,000.

Let 10–20 percent of the nutrient solution drain from the growing medium after each irrigation cycle to help maintain EC stability. The runoff carries away any excess fertilizer salt buildup in the growing medium.

10–20%

Bad Water

If the raw irrigation water has a reading of more than 300 ppm, or the sodium level is above 50 ppm, or the calcium/magnesium levels make water "hard," you should use a reverse osmosis device to filter the mineral salts and make "pure" water.

Salt buildup, as seen on this showerhead, is a problem when using hard water (sodium chloride) or other mineral-laden water.

Gardens that suffer from sodium-rich water will never reach full harvest potential.

Reverse osmosis (RO) filters are the easiest and most efficient means to clean excess minerals (dissolved solids) from raw water. To use an RO filter, you need a water tap, drain, and reservoir for the "clean" water. About 65–70 percent of the water processed is waste, and 30–35 percent clean water with an EC near 0.

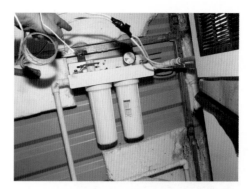

Moving Water

A readily accessible water source saves time and labor. A 4 × 4-foot (1.2 × 1.2 m) garden containing 16 healthy plants in 3-gallon (11 L) pots needs 10–25 gallons (40–100 L) of water per week. Water weighs 8 pounds per gallon (1 kg/L). Run a hose to the garden. A lightweight half-inch (1.5 cm) hose is easy to handle. The hose should have an on/off valve at the outlet. A rigid water wand (see www.rainwand.com) will save many broken branches while watering in tight quarters.

Fill a watering container with water and nutrients and irrigate by hand if no other source of water is available. Watering by hand is simple and efficient. It also puts you in direct contact with plants.

Maintaining the proper nutrient solution water/fertilizer balance at the right temperature range and keeping the growing medium evenly moist and aerated are the keys to successful hydroponic gardening.

Drip systems are used in soil or hydroponic gardens. They deliver nutrient solution (stored in a reservoir) one drop at a time or in low volume, via a low-pressure plastic pipe with friction fittings. Water flows down the pipe and out the emitter one drop at a time or at a very slow rate. The emitters attached to the main hose are either spaghetti tubes or a nozzle dripper actually emitting from the main hose. Drip irrigation kits are available at garden stores and building centers.

Once set up, drip systems reduce watering maintenance. Fertilizer may also be applied easily via the irrigation system.

A drip system attached to a timer disperses nutrient solution at regular intervals. Do not leave a drip system on its own for more than 4 consecutive days, or you could return to a surprise!

Draining Water

Marijuana does not like dry or soggy soil. Soil kept too wet drowns the roots, squeezing out oxygen necessary for nutrient absorption. If soil is too dry foliage does not have enough water. Either case causes slow growth and possible fungal attacks. Poor drainage is most often the cause of soggy soil. It is compounded by poor ventilation and high humidity.

You will have to drain much water out of your grow room. Water can go down a drain or be caught and pumped or carried away. A floor drain is the easiest method but not always practical or available. Catching drain water in a reservoir requires plants to be elevated on a table. Once the drain water is directed back to the drain basin, it can be removed by hand or with a pump.

Excess irrigation water is carried away by a floor drain.

Cover soil with clay pellets to help keep soil surface moist.

Leaching soil flushes out excess nutrient salts that build up in the soil. Flushing the bad stuff out of the soil prevents many possible problems. To leach, put a plant into a deep sink, bathtub, or over a bucket, and then water heavily with three times the volume of water as soil in the pot.

Hydroponics

Hydroponics stores make their money selling you hydroponic systems. The salespeople are knowledgeable and can tell you a lot about the systems they sell, but they may oversell their products, and you could end up buying things you do not need. When you consider purchasing hydroponics, start out slowly and purchase a system that can be expanded. Most systems require that you measure the pH and EC (ppm) of the nutrient solution as well as turn it on and off automatically, which requires a timer. Other than that, you will not need more fancy instruments and cool gadgets. Get as much experience as possible before investing too heavily.

Growing hydroponically is considered by many to be superior to growing in soil because you can give plants maximum levels of the exact nutrients they need. Precise control of nutrient uptake makes it possible to reap higher yields faster.

Soilless mix in three-gallon pots supports this dense crop of buds. I like soilless mixes because they are easy to control.

One of the most productive ways to grow marijuana hydroponically is in pots full of soilless mix because it is simple, easy, and forgiving.

**Advantages
of Hydroponic Gardens**

- Clean
- High yields
- Maximize nutrient levels
- Precise nutrient control
- Faster growth
- No soil to change

**Disadvantages
of Hydroponic Gardens**

- Can be expensive
- Can be complicated
- Some systems are unforgiving
- Can be difficult to set up and
  control
- Need pH and EC electronic meters

Nutrient Solutions

To avoid problems, change the nutrient solution in the reservoir every week. Change nutrient solution every two weeks in systems with a large reservoir. You may need to change the nutrient solution more often when plants are in the last stages of flowering because they use more nutrients at that time.

Plants use so much water that nutrient solutions need to be replenished regularly. Water is used at a much faster rate than nutrients. Casually "topping off" the reservoir with pH-balanced water will keep the solution relatively balanced for a week or two. Some growers top off the nutrient solution with 500–700 ppm-strength nutrient solution every 2–3 days. Never let the nutrient solution go for more than 4 weeks before draining it and adding fresh solution. Smart growers avoid problems and leach the entire system with weak nutrient solution for an hour or more between changing the reservoir.

Check EC of reservoir, growing medium, and runoff nutrient solution at the same time every day. Use an electronic EC pen to monitor the level of dissolved solids in the solution.

The smaller the reservoir, the more rapid the depletion and the more critical it is to keep it full. Smaller reservoirs should be refilled daily.

Humic and fulvic acids chelate metallic ions, making them readily transportable by water. The (fertilizer) micronutrients—copper, iron, manganese, and zinc—are difficult to dissolve. When mixed in a chelated form, they become readily available for absorption.

Hydroponic Systems

Passive hydroponic systems rely on capillary action to transfer the nutrient solution "passively" from the reservoir to the growing medium. The Dutch are masters of passive systems and achieve amazing results. Wick systems have no moving parts. Low initial cost and low maintenance enhance wick systems' popularity.

Passive hydroponic garden

Active hydroponic systems "actively" move the nutrient solution, which is usually recovered. Cannabis is a fast-growing plant and very well suited to active hydroponic systems.

Ebb and flow (flood and drain) **hydroponic systems** are low maintenance and easy to use. Individual plants in pots or rockwool cubes are set on a special growing bed table that can hold 1–4 inches (3–10 cm) of nutrient solution. Nutrient solution is pumped into the table or growing bed. The rockwool blocks or containers are flooded from the bottom, which pushes the oxygen-poor air out. Once the nutrient solution reaches a set level, an overflow pipe drains the excess to the reservoir. Ebb and flow systems are ideal for growing many short plants in a Sea of Green garden. A Sea of Green garden is comprised of short females growing closely together, imitating a sea of green. Any garden with plants grouped closely together can be considered a sea of green. Many gardens in this book fit the criteria for sea of green but are not so labeled.

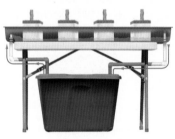

Ebb and flow hydroponic garden

In **deep water culture** (DWC), seedlings and clones are held in net pots full of expanded clay pellets, rockwool, or other growing mediums. These pots are nestled in holes in a lid that covers the reservoir. Roots dangle into the nutrient solution. A submersible pump lifts nutrient solution to where it splashes into the access lid wetting roots. Roots easily absorb nutrients and water from the solution in the oxygenated environment. An air stone pumps in more bubbles of oxygen. Gardens are low maintenance and simple by design, and require no timer because the pumps are on 24 hours a day.

DWC hydroponic garden

Top-feed hydroponic systems meter nutrient solution in specific doses via spaghetti tubing or an emitter placed at the base of individual plants. Aerated nutrient solution flows into the growing medium and is taken up by roots. The runoff nutrient solution is directed back to the reservoir as soon as it drains from the growing medium.

Top-feed systems come in many configurations. Systems with several gallons (20–25 liters) of growing medium are best for growing large plants that may require support. Small containers are perfect for smaller plants.

Top-feed hydroponic garden

Top-feed systems can be
- Single buckets
- Multiple bucket
- Coco or rockwool slabs in individual trays
- Tables of coco or rockwool slabs
- Individual blocks
- Vertical systems

Rockwool, gravel, coconut coir, and expanded clay are the most common growing mediums found in top-feed systems. Versatile top-feed systems can be used with individual containers or slabs in individual beds or lined up on tables.

NFT hydroponic garden

Aeroponic garden

Nutrient film technique (NFT) hydroponic systems are high-performance gardens when fine-tuned. Aerated nutrient solution flows to roots located in gulleys. Seedlings or cuttings with a strong root system are placed on capillary matting located on the bottom in a covered channel. The capillary matting stabilizes nutrient solution flow and holds roots in place. Constantly aerated nutrient solution flows down the channel or gulley, over and around the roots and back to the reservoir. Irrigation is most often constant, 24 hours a day. Roots receive plenty of oxygen and are able to absorb a maximum of nutrient solution. Proper gulley incline, volume, and flow of nutrient solution are key elements in NFT gardens.

Aeroponic systems use no growing medium and offer the highest performance possible. Roots are suspended in a dark growth chamber with no growing medium. Roots are misted with oxygen-rich nutrient solution at regular intervals. The humidity in the chamber remains at or near 100 percent 24 hours a day. Roots have the maximum potential to absorb nutrient in the presence of air.

Reservoirs

Nutrient solution reservoirs should be as big as possible and have a lid to reduce evaporation. Gardens use from 5–25 percent of the nutrient solution every day. A large volume of nutrient solution will minimize nutrient imbalances.

Add water as soon as the solution level drops. The reservoir should contain at least 25 percent more nutrient solution than it takes to fill the beds to compensate for daily use and evaporation.

Check the level of the reservoir daily, and replenish if necessary. Use an indelible marker to make a full line and write the number of gallons or liters contained at that point on the inside of the reservoir tank. Use this volume measure when mixing nutrients.

Maintaining the nutrient solution temperature around 60°F (15°C) will help control transpiration and humidity. It will also promote the uptake of nutrients.

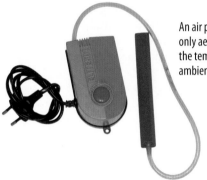

An air pump submerged in the reservoir not only aerates the solution, it helps level out the temperature differential between ambient air and reservoir.

Soil & Soilless Mixes

Soil and soilless mixes that look like soil but are inert are my favorite growing mediums. They are inexpensive, easy to use, and forgiving. Maybe it is just my prejudice, but as a lifelong gardener, I like to get my hands dirty.

Advantages of soil gardens
- Sweet organic taste
- Forgiving to growers
- Simple and easy

Disadvantages of soil gardens
- Must move soil in and out
- Slower growth
- Can be messy

Potting Soil

Potting soil fresh out of the bag often fulfils all requirements for a growing medium: texture that allows good root penetration, water retention, and drainage; a stable pH between 6 and 7; and a minimum supply of nutrients. The best choice is a premium fast-draining soil with good texture that will not break down quickly.

Use a potting soil only once. Depleted used soil has poor water and air retention causing compaction and reduced drainage. Some growers mix their old potting soil with new potting soil to stretch their mix. Cutting corners this way most often costs more in production losses than is saved in soil.

Soilless Mixes

Soilless mixes are popular, inexpensive, lightweight, inert, and sterile growing mediums. Premixed commercial soilless mixes are an excellent value. They retain moisture and air while allowing good drainage, strong root penetration, and even growth. Fertilizer concentration, moisture level, and pH are very easy to control. Unless fortified with nutrient, soilless mixes contain no nutrients and are pH balanced near 6.0 to 7.0.

Soil Mixes

Indoors soil mixes can be messy and a lot of work. It is much easier to buy good potting soil and mix in about 10–15 percent perlite and some form of micronutrient and trichoderma bacteria that causes roots to absorb nutrients better. Do not use backyard soil. Do not reuse soil unless it is totally clean. Avert problems with soil mixes by purchasing all the components.

Add to potting soil	Soil mixes with store-bought mushroom compost	
15% perlite	50% compost	50% compost
25% coco peat	50% soilless mix	50% coco coir
Trichoderma		
Trace elements	33% compost	33% compost
	33% soilless mix	33% soilless mix
	33% coco coir	16% worm castings
		16% perlite

Mix soil thoroughly before planting and lightly cultivate the surface to increase water penetration.

CHAPTER 10

Grow Cabinets, Closets, and Rooms

INTRODUCTION

This chapter is where you put it all together to set up your grow room(s) and cultivate the best crop in the world! Before you set up the room, you will need to determine how much to grow. Afterward you must decide on the location, size, and your budget. Of course, you will need tools and construction supplies to set up the room.

The size of the grow room will dictate how much you can grow. Size depends upon your personal needs and desires. The size of the grow space dictates the type, wattage, and number of lamps. The most efficient lights with the highest lumens-per-watt conversion include CFLs and HIDs.

Once 6 to 18-inch-tall (9–45 cm) plants are in the flowering room, they will produce from 0.5–1.0 gram of buds per watt of light every 60 days—if everything goes according to plan. For example, with 200 watts of light in the flowering room you should harvest from 100–200 grams (3.5–7 oz) of dried buds at the end of 60 days if all goes well. A 400-watt lamp will yield from 200–400 grams (7–14 oz). See table below for more information.

APPROXIMATE HARVEST OF DRIED BUDS		
after 60–70 days of flowering		
WATTS	GRAMS	OUNCES
200	100–200	3.5–7.0
400	200–400	7.0–14
600	300–600	10.5–21
800	400–800	14–28
1000	500–1000	17.5–35

Location

The location of the grow room sets the stage for the water, air, growing system, and lights in the grow room. The essentials include a convenient electrical outlet to supply power to the room, and an air exhaust outlet—preferably one that goes outside the building—to vent the exhaust air from the grow room(s).

We will look at some of the differences between the following locations: basement, attic, ground floor, and outbuilding.

A **basement** is a great location for a grow space. The temperature and humidity are usually easy to keep constant. Concrete walls backed with soil serve as insulation. Some basements lend themselves to construction of a false wall. You can also locate the door to the grow room in the back of a closet or below a workbench. A trapdoor to the basement covered by a rug or table is also stealthy!

Attic grow spaces often have trouble with heat buildup because heat rises and congregates there. If the roof is not insulated, the garden may suffer from cold in the winter and high temperatures in the summer. However, many attics are difficult to access, which cuts casual traffic and the chance of discovery.

Outbuildings, garages, and barns not attached to homes are some of the worst places to grow cannabis. Cops and robbers can get into these structures easier; security is much better when the entry to the garden is within another building. The grow room located in this outbuilding was raided by Dutch police a few months after this photo was snapped.

Main-floor grow rooms located in closets, cabinets, bedrooms, and spare rooms are very common. These rooms are easy to access, which is good for maintenance and bad for security. The atmosphere is usually easy to regulate because it is controlled along with the temperature and humidity of the home.

Budget

Next you must budget for grow room construction. Here is an approximate budget of what a simple closet grow room would cost to construct. If you are on a super tight budget, you can shave the numbers by scrounging and buying secondhand equipment. Of course costs will vary depending upon prices in your area and the components in the grow closet.

Refer to Constructing a Grow Closet, page 135 for complete instructions on building a closet grow room.

BUDGET FOR GROW ROOM ESSENTIALS			
	NORMAL	**CHEAP**	**CHEAPEST**
Grow lights	$300	$200	$ 50
Ventilation fan	$100	$ 50	$ 50
Circulation fan	$ 40	$ 30	$ 20
Charcoal filter	$200	$200	$ 50
Thermo/hygrometer	$ 30	$ 30	$ 30
White walls	$ 30	$ 20	$ 0
Containers	$ 10	$ 0	$ 0
Soil or soilless mix	$ 20	$ 20	$ 20
Tools	$100	$ 50	$ 0
Fertilizer	$ 30	$ 30	$ 30
Construction supplies	$110	$ 50	$ 10
TOTAL	**$970**	**$680**	**$260**

Constructing a Grow Closet

Tools

Here are a few tools you will need to set up your grow room.
I like to use both hand and power tools when appropriate.

Tools Normally Needed

Saws—Japanese
Electric drill
Battery-powered screwdriver
Hammer
Putty knife
Tape measure

Supplies Normally Needed

Screw—sheetrock
Screws/nuts—for Mecalux
Screws—butterfly
Caulk
Cable ties
Duct tape
Visqueen plastic for walls
Velcro
1 × 1 m plywood for ceiling

Battery-charged electric
screwdriver with a complete
array of driver heads

Cable ties make fastening as
easy as a tug and click.

Set of drill bits for wood, metal, and ceramic

Electric drill

Claw hammer

Two saws: one (flat) for cutting boards and one for cutting holes. You can also use a power saw.

Several hooks to hang lamps, cords, timers, etc.

Indelible marking pens to mark distances and identify plants

Pliers to grip and hold

Ceramic and wood screws

Butterfly bolt

Measuring tape

Teflon tape to seal treads and prevent moisture leaks

Velcro to seal doors and section off rooms

Step-by-Step: Construction

STEP ONE: Design Room

Once you know how much you want to grow and where you want to grow, you are ready to design your grow room or purchase a ready-made room. I like to draw the room to scale on paper before constructing it.

This room has a single growing space that measures 3 × 3 feet (90 × 90 cm) and contains plants and a 400-watt HID lamp. A space above contains electrical appliances including the ballast for the lamp. A space below the growing bed serves as a storage area. This is a good garden design for beginners who start with feminized seeds. They can start growing immediately and harvest in about 4 months. Harvest should weigh in between 7–14 ounces (200–400 gm) at the end of 4 months.

400-watt lamp	150-watt fan
15-watt timer	560 total watts

This grow closet is divided by a shelf just below the middle. The seedling/vegetative/clone mother garden below is illuminated by two 55-watt CFL bulbs. The flowering room above is illuminated by a 400-watt HP sodium lamp. This room offers growers the option of

[*Description continues next page*]

400-watt lamp	150-watt vent fan
110-watt CFL	100-watt fan
15-watt timer	775 total watts

consecutive harvests every 60–70 days. Seedlings or clones and mothers are grown below. Seedlings or clones advance into strong vegetative growth and are moved upstairs to the flowering room every 60–70 days, after ripe buds are harvested. This room requires a little more knowledge and care but is very productive. Growers should expect to harvest about 7–14 ounces (200–400 gm) every 60–70 days from this garden.

NOTE: This setup also offers growers the option of a perpetual harvest. A single flowering plant is harvested every 2–4 days. Mothers and clones are grown in the vegetative room below. Clones advance into strong vegetative growth and a vegetative clone is moved to the flowering room every time a flowering plant is harvested. This room takes a little more knowledge but is very productive. Growers should expect to harvest about 20 percent more with this rhythm method.

If you set up two rooms, one for seedlings, vegetative growth, or mothers and clones and another room for flowering, you can harvest a crop of ripe buds every 60–70 days. The light is on in the clone/vegetative room 18–24 hours a day and the flowering room has a light schedule of 12 hours on and 12 hours off. To get the most from your space, the flowering room should be 3–4 times bigger than the clone/vegetative room. For example, a 2 × 2-foot (60 × 60 cm) clone/vegetative room will supply enough seedlings and clones to support up to an 8 × 8-foot (2.4 × 2.4 m) flowering room. Or you can use the grow closet like the one on the front cover of this book as an example. With two rooms and this simple schedule, you can harvest 5–6 crops of dried buds every year.

This grow setup also has two grow rooms: clone/vegetative and flowering. A 400-watt lamp illuminates the flowering room and four 40-watt fluorescents light the clone/ vegetative room. The side-by-side orientation of the rooms allows the vegetative room to be taller and narrower and the closet a little wider. The higher profile of the flowering room allows space for a hydroponic reservoir below. It also provides space above and below for appliances and storage.

400-watt lamp	200-watt fan
160-watt fluorescents	100-watt fan
15-watt timer	875 total watts

STEP TWO: Assess electrical needs

The average small 1- or 2-room grow closet will need a single 15–20 amp electrical circuit at 120 volts and a 10–15 amp circuit at 240 volts. An electrical circuit is considered overloaded when it is at 80 percent capacity. For example, a 15-amp circuit is overloaded when it draws 12 amps and a 20-amp circuit is overloaded at 16 amps. As you can see, all the circuits below are well below overload.

Refer to *Marijuana Horticulture: The Indoor/ Outdoor Medical Grower's Bible* for more information on electrical circuits in larger grow rooms.

VOLTS	×	AMPS	=	WATTS
120	×	7.3	=	876
120	×	4.7	=	564
120	×	6.5	=	780

VOLTS	×	AMPS	=	WATTS
240	×	3.65	=	876
240	×	2.35	=	564
240	×	3.25	=	780

NOTE: All electrical outlets and plugs require a ground wire for safety. Ground wires are either green or brown, or brown with a green stripe.

UK electrical plug   EU electrical plug   USA electrical plug

APPLIANCE	AMPERES AT **120** VOLTS	AMPERES AT **240** VOLTS
100-watt lamp	0.85	0.43
250-watt lamp	2.2	1.1
400-watt lamp	3.4	1.7
600-watt lamp	6	2.5
1000-watt lamp	8.8	4.4
100-watt circulation fan	0.85	0.43
150-watt vent fan	1.2	0.6
50-watt pump	0.42	0.21

(All ampere values are approximate)

GFI outlet

You will also need an easy-to-access electrical outlet. Ideally, the outlet should be inside the room. Remember to keep water away from the outlet. You also might want to install a ground fault interrupter (GFI) outlet with its own breaker switch. If you must run an extension cord from the outlet to the room, make sure the wire for the extension cord is at least 16/3 (16 gauge wire with 3 strands, one of which is grounded) or it will lose voltage enroute. Do not let the run of the electrical cord go more than 10 feet (3 m)—the shorter the better.

European breaker boxes control 240 volts of electricity at 50 cycles.

Circuit breaker box showing 20-, 50-, and 100-amp breakers

This large circuit box from a North American garden is full of breaker switches that meter 120 volts of electricity at 60 cycles to a home with a grow room.

STEP THREE: Enclose the room

Can't make holes in walls? Build a freestanding garden.

If you are lucky, you already have a small, enclosed room; if not, it is easy to enclose a room so that you can control everything inside. However, many growers choose to set up a grow area in an unused corner of a larger room. There are many examples of partially enclosed and unenclosed grow rooms in Chapter 11.

Mecalux angle iron with holes provides an easy construction support for walls and shelves.

Enclose a grow room by framing it with boards, usually 2 × 4s (5 × 10 cm), or use Mecalux (see photo on the right). Once the superstructure is set up, cover it with Visqueen plastic, plywood, or Sheetrock. The room's finish on the outside depends upon your security needs. Rooms covered with Visqueen are difficult to keep a secret. Rooms with rigid walls are generally easier to control and contain light and odors.

Enclose the room with white Visqueen plastic. Secure plastic to walls with staples, screw down 1 × 2-inch strips with Sheetrock screws, or duct tape. Join seams together with duct tape.

Insulating the room will help contain sound and help control temperature and humidity.

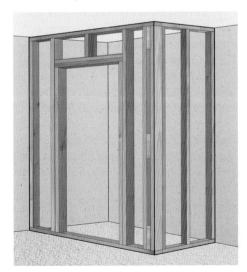

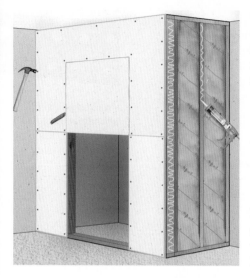

Cover the outside walls with Sheetrock once it is insulated. Sheetrock will further deaden the sound and make the room blend in with the rest of the rooms in the home.

Install a door with a lock and key. Make sure to line the perimeter of the door with plastic or carpet to help contain light and sound inside the grow room.

STEP FOUR: Divide Room

Divide the room to make a seedling/clone/mother/vegetative room on the bottom third and a flowering room on top. Install a plywood shelf to form a partition between the top and bottom of the grow closet.

Frame 1 × 2-inch (3 × 5 cm) boards or Mecalux, 3–3.5 feet (90–100 cm) from the floor around the walls of the room. Secure 1 × 2-inch (3 × 5 cm) boards with screws. Cut a 3 × 4-foot (90 × 120 cm) piece of 0.75-inch (1.9 cm) plywood with a 6 × 6-inch (15 cm²) piece cut from the right rear corner for the duct vent. Set the plywood on the ledge of the 1 × 2-inch (3 × 5 cm) boards with the vent hole toward the back wall.

Install rigid 6-inch (15 cm) ducting through the hole to connect the vegetative and flowering rooms. Use small screws to install a small inline fan in the pipe to direct air up from the vegetative room to the flowering room.

STEP FIVE: Whiteout Room and Line Floor with Plastic

Reflective walls increase light coverage on the perimeter of a garden about 10 percent. Paint the ceiling and walls white or cover them with white Visqueen plastic, reflective Mylar, or a similar product. Use high-quality semigloss white latex paint. Do not use inexpensive paint because it takes longer to apply. Use a roller and paintbrush to apply paint.

Cover the floor with heavy plastic to form a large tray to protect the floor from dirt and water. Fold the plastic so that at least 6 inches (15 cm) run up the wall. Attach the plastic floor covering to the walls with duct tape or staples.

STEP SIX: Install a Vent Fan

A vent fan is necessary in virtually all grow rooms. See Air Ventilation and Air Ducting in Chapter 9 for more information. Most grow rooms require some sort of odor control (see Step Seven, page 146) to keep it secure from cops and robbers. In this case, the fan will need to be more powerful to draw air through a charcoal filter if one is used to clean the air.

Often one of the biggest obstacles to constructing a grow room is where and how to run the exit ducting with a minimum of work and structural damage.

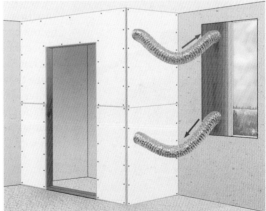

Construct a ventilation system that brings in cool air to the bottom of the room and expels hot air from the top of the room.

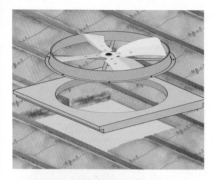

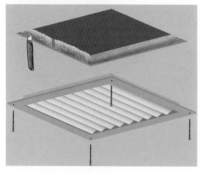

Normally you can run the vent out a window, chimney, sewer vent, or other pre-existing exit. Locate the vent in the ceiling or near the ceiling where hot air naturally accumulates. Carefully cut a hole in the wall or ceiling and in the exact place you want it. Smart growers plan the entire project on paper before cutting holes in existing structures.

Use rigid ducting instead of flexible ducting if possible. The larger the ducting the more freely and quietly air will flow out. Choose between 4-, 6-, 8-, 10-, and 12-inch (10, 15, 20, 25, 30 cm) ducting.

If cutting into a ceiling with a crawl space, make sure you have a method to evacuate the grow room air from the crawl space. Install louvers below the rafters on the outside wall of the house.

Cut the hole in the ceiling into the attic or directly through the roof. Go into the attic and measure where the hole will come out. Make sure there are no wires or other impediments before cutting the hole. Pull back insulation above the hole if necessary. Use the ducting or the fan to mark a circle where you want to make the hole. Drill a 1-inch hole near the center of the circle. Use a hand hole saw to cut out the circle just outside the line. Install the vent fan and supply it with electricity. Hide the fan with louvers attached to the ceiling.

Install a vent in the attic

Roof fan interior

Cutting a hole in the roof could cause leaks later. Think before acting and make sure you know what you are doing.

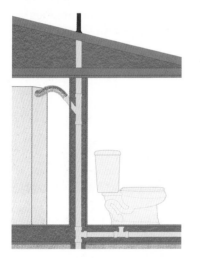

Run ventilation ducting into the chimney.

Tap into ABS plastic sewer drain vents and insert the extraction vent. Make sure that you are tapping into the ventilation pipe rather than the actual sewer pipe. Install a backflow vent in the extraction duct so that foul-smelling odors do not invade the grow room.

NOTE: Before completing any of these jobs, discuss the project with a professional at the building supply store. The author and the publisher do not take any responsibility whatsoever for damages that may be caused by installing ventilation.

Carbon air filter

Check with the web sites listed at right to select the proper filter and extraction fan for your room. Remember, drawing air through an extraction carbon filter will require a larger extraction fan than specified under Air Ventilation in Chapter 9.

STEP SEVEN: Neutralize Odors

Neutralize the fragrance of flowering marijuana before air is vented from the grow room so that odors do not cause security problems. The most popular and effective method is to use an activated charcoal filter attached to a vent fan.

Unless made from new lightweight carbon-impregnated material, carbon filters can be quite heavy and require stout mounting. Make sure to choose the right one for your grow area so you don't have to mount a filter that is too heavy. For example, a carbon filter rated at 200 cfm is more than adequate for the average closet grow room.

See www.carbonactive.eu for information on great new lightweight carbon filters.

Check www.hydroasis.com for information about the lightweight Organic Air Charcoal Fiber Filter.

Check www.canfilters.com for more on Can-Filters. These are the best-selling activated charcoal filters, but they are quite heavy.

It is also a good idea to mask any lingering odors with a strong air freshener or a host of odor masking products. Check with your local hydroponic store for more information on such products. Search "hydroponic store" on www.google.com.

STEP EIGHT:
Install a Circulation Fan

Air circulation is necessary in all grow rooms, especially during flowering. Usually air circulation must be increased with a circulation fan or fans. Small clip-on oscillating fans come in very handy to circulate air in small grow rooms. They are easy to move and direct air where needed. Or you can mount an inexpensive oscillating fan to the ceiling or buy an actual wall-mounted fan. See the fan size table in Chapter 9 to help you choose the proper circulation fan(s) for your room.

Wall-mounted circulation fan

In general rooms require at least one 12-inch (30 cm) circulation fan for every 400 watts of light.

Fan mounted with bungee cords

STEP NINE:
Install a Thermometer/Hygrometer

Install at least one maximum/ minimum thermometer/hygrometer in your grow room to measure temperature and humidity. I prefer the digital models because they are relatively accurate and easy to use. Calibrate them against 1 or 2 other thermometer/hygrometers so they remain accurate. Place the thermometer/hygrometer equidistant between the ceiling and floor, and fasten to the wall or hang from a string. Check the meter daily.

Clip-on circulation fan

You can control the climate in most grow rooms with a vent fan attached to a timer or a rheostat. See Air Temperature and Humidity in Chapter 9 for more information. Personally inspecting the meter and plants daily will help you gain experience and learn exactly how much ventilation the room needs to keep the temperature about 75°F (24°C) day and 65°–70°F (18°–21°C) at night and the humidity below

50 percent (day/night) in the flowering room, and the vegetative room at 75°F (24°C) day and 65°–70°F (18°–21°C) at night and 60 percent humidity both day and night.

If you have the extra money to invest, you may want to invest in one of the many controllers available to control temperature and humidity. Prices range from $80–$1,500 USD. Smart growers buy quality controllers even though they cost a few dollars more.

Check these sites for more information on atmospheric controllers:

www.greenair.com
www.hydrofarm.com
www.sunlightsupply.com

Max/min thermometer

Temperature controller

Atmospheric controller

STEP TEN: Set Up Lights

Orient the reflective hood fixture so that light shines most efficiently. Less light shines from the ends of the fixture and more from the sides, thus throwing a rectangular foot-print of light below. For example, if the room is 3 × 4 feet (90 × 120 cm), orient the HID fixture so that the ends of the bulb run on the 3-foot (90 cm) axis and the sides along the 4-foot (120 cm) axis.

Hang the lamp from an eyebolt.

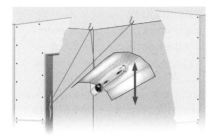

Orientation of lamp and reflector for best light coverage

To install a lamp in the flowering room, insert 1 or 2 hooks depending upon light fixture requirements in a secure portion such as a beam or 2 × 4 (5 × 10 cm) board of the ceiling. Mount the HID reflective hood/bulb fixture attaching it to the hook(s) with chain or cord. If using cord, attach the other end to a cleat on the wall so that it is easy to move the fixture up and down.

Set the remote ballast outside the grow room or on a shelf near the ceiling so that excess heat will stay high in the room and be easy to evacuate.

If ballast is attached to the fixture, hooks should be strong enough to support 30 pounds (14 kg) for each lamp.

Install smaller lights in the vegetative/clone/seedling room. Screw hooks into the 0.75-inch (1.9 cm) plywood lower ceiling and to hang fluorescent, CFL, or HID fixtures. Hang from adjustable chains or cords. Attach the other end of cords to a cleat on the wall.

Turn on the lights!

STEP ELEVEN: Room Systems Check

Now the room is all set up, make a test to ensure that every-thing operates properly before introducing plants. Turn everything on—lights, fans, etc. to make sure they all work at the same time. Set a large pan of water out on the main growing beds to simulate plant transpiration. Close the doors of the grow room and let everything run for an hour or two. Open the doors and check the temperature and humidity in the room. Next turn off the fans and let the light run for 30 minutes with the doors closed. Check the temperature and humidity levels to see if the room is hotter and more humid with no ventilation.

Check the hydroponic garden before adding plants. Cycle all the systems to ensure that water flows from all emitters and runs back to the nutrient tank unobstructed. Check for leaks. Cycle the timer on/off functions several times while you are watching the system to ensure everything works properly.

STEP TWELVE: Move in Plants

Move seedlings and rooted clones into the room. Huddle them closely together under the lamp. Make sure the HID is not so close to small plants that it burns their leaves. Position 400-watt lamps 18 inches (45 cm) above seedlings and clones. Place a 600-watt lamp 24 inches (60 cm) away and a 1000-watt lamp 30 inches (75 cm) away. Check the distance daily. Hang a precut string from the hood to measure distance.

Enjoy!

Move in plants!

Growing in the Room

Growing in your newly constructed grow room is easy once you have it set up and have a simple weekly plan to follow. The examples below give you a 12-week guideline showing you how big plants should be and what to do and when. It will also show you when the most common problems occur. When you can anticipate problems, they are much easier to avoid. The "week" starts on Monday and ends on Sunday. First let's start with a little background on good and bad grow habits.

Physically check every aspect of your garden daily.

Good growing will be rewarded with big, strong plants.

Any mistakes that cause plants to suffer stress will retard growth and diminish harvest.

Strain

The strain could be any medium-growing *indica/sativa* cross such as Jorge's Diamonds #1, Bidi Early, Flo, Romulan, Skunk Kush, etc. Most growers choose a strain that normally comes ripe 8 weeks after inducing flowering.

NOTE: In general *indica*-dominant strains can take higher fertilizer concentrations than *sativa*-dominant strains.

California Orange

Bidi Early

Flo

Romulan

Skunk Kush

Jorge's Diamonds #1

Clones or Seedlings

Clones take 11 weeks (3 weeks vegetative, 8 weeks flowering) from the time rooted clones are introduced into the vegetative room.

Seedlings take 14–15 weeks (4 weeks seedling, 3 vegetative, 8 flowering) from the time seeds are planted into the vegetative room.

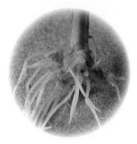

Roots grow in 10–14 days.

NOTE: Seedlings must grow longer, 8 weeks total, from the time cotyledon leaves appear.

Light

Vegetative growth time is 3 weeks for best production. Light schedule is 18 hours on, 6 off (or 24 on 0 off)

Flowering time is 8 weeks for most strains. Light schedule is 12 hours on, 12 off.

This example assumes you are growing 20 plants under 400-watt lamp(s). The lamp is kept 12–30 inches (30–75 cm) above plants.

Atmosphere

Adequate air ventilation and circulation are installed to keep the room temperature and humidity level at the desired levels noted every week.

NOTE: Incoming air should be about the same temperature as air inside the room. Circulation fans should not blow directly on plants.

Soil or Hydroponics

You can grow in hydroponics or soil. Hydroponic gardens usually grow faster than soil gardens.

Size of Container

Soil & soilless mixes:
3-gallon (11 L) containers

Hydroponics: follow manufacturer's guidelines for the system. In general, top off reservoir daily.

Use a soil or soilless mix that drains freely and still holds plenty of water.

Water

Water is assumed to be relatively clean with few contaminants and low levels of dissolved solids (mineral salts). If your local water tastes bad, check the analysis with your water company. You can usually do it on the Internet.

NOTE: Fast-growing plants could dry out daily after the sixth week.

NOTE: Irrigate containers so that 10%–20% runs off as drainage. This will flush out any built-up fertilizer salts in the growing medium. Do not leave plants in standing water.

pH

6–6.5 pH soil
5.5 pH hydroponics

Fertilizer

- Do start with a high quality (hydroponic) fertilizer, organic or chemical.
- Do start and stay with the same brand of fertilizer and additives.
- Do follow the instructions provided by the fertilizer manufacturer.
- Do NOT overfeed plants! Overfertilizing is one of the most common problems. Follow directions!
- Do NOT listen to friends who are not growers or somebody with no experience.
- No specific brands of fertilizer or additives are recommended.

NOTE: pH recommendations are given for soil and hydroponics, but follow the pH recommendations of the fertilizer manufacturer.

Overfertilized plant

Twelve Week Grow Scenario

WEEK ONE: First Week of Vegetative Growth

Light/dark: 18 hours day, 6 hours night
Light intensity: 400-watt lamp to 24–30 inches (60–75 cm) above tender plants. Note: other HID and CFL lamps can also be used. Check Chapter 9 for specifications.
Temperature: 75°F (24°C) day, 72°F (22°C) night
Humidity: 60% day, 60% night
pH: 6–6.5 pH soil, 5.5 pH hydroponics

Move clones or seedlings in 1-pint (55 cl) 4-inch pots into the room. Plants should be about 4–6 inches (10–15 cm) tall. Drawing above is a seedling.

Water: Keep growing medium evenly moist so that roots stay wet but still have enough oxygen to take in nutrients. Be very careful not to overwater the limited number of roots or let tender roots dry out. Irrigate with enough water so that 10%–20% flows out the bottom of the container. Do not let plants sit in standing water.
Do: Keep growing medium evenly moist
Don't: Overwater and make soggy soil

Fertilizer: Use your favorite "grow" nutrients for seedlings and use as per manufacturer's instructions. Use any additives suggested by the manufacturer.

Growth Characteristics: During the first week of vegetative growth, plants develop a strong root system. You will see signs of upward green growth too. Now it is very important to keep plants from suffering water and temperature stress. Be careful and water only as needed.

Strong root system.

Seedlings get off to a slow start, but once established, growth is very rapid.

This plant is 8 days old.

Once clones are rooted, they can be moved into the vegetative room. Keep the growing medium evenly moist whether they are in soil or a hydroponic system.

Clean room regularly and wash your hands before touching plants.

WEEK TWO: Second Week of Vegetative Growth

During the second week, plants should be about 6–8 inches (15–20 cm) tall.

Light/dark: 18 hours day, 6 hours night
Light intensity: 400-watt lamp to 24–30 inches (60–75 cm) above tender plants
Temperature: 75°F (24°C) day, 72°F (22°C) night
Humidity: 60% day, 60% night
pH: 6–6.5 pH soil, 5.5 pH hydroponics

Water: Plants need a little more water now. Keep growing medium evenly moist. Be very careful not to overwater or let tender roots dry out.

Fertilizer: Use your favorite "grow" nutrients with higher levels of nitrogen for green growth as per instructions. Add any additives suggested by the company.

Growth Characteristics: During the second week of vegetative growth plants will continue to develop strong root systems, and green leafy growth increases notably. Now it is very important to keep plants from suffering water and temperature stress.

Plants need a little more water now.

Water small clones and seedlings regularly, and keep the growing medium evenly moist.

If light does not penetrate foliage, and bottom leaves yellow as plants grow taller, remove them. Remove bottom pair of leaves especially if they show signs of weak growth.

Leafy growth increases.

WEEK THREE: Third Week of Vegetative Growth

During the third week, plants should be about 10–12 inches (25–30 cm) tall.

Light/dark: 18 hours day, 6 hours night
Light intensity: 400-watt lamp to 24 inches (60 cm) above plants
Temperature: 75°F (24°C) day, 72°F (22°C) night
Humidity: 60% day, 60% night
pH: 6–6.5 pH soil, 5.5 pH hydroponics

Water: Plants need 16 ounces (500 ml) or more of water per week. Keep growing medium evenly moist. Continue to monitor water levels carefully to avoid overwatering and underwatering.

Flush on Friday of the last week of vegetative growth. Plants will need a good flushing to wash out any built up nitrogen in the growing medium. Leach plants in 4-inch pots with 3 times the volume of water as the volume of growing medium to wash out any built-up nitrogen in the growing medium. For example, flush a 4-inch, one-pint (50 cl) container with 3 pints (150 cl) of water.

0.5 quart

0.5 liter

Transplant: On Sunday, transplant clones and seedlings into 3-gallon (11 L) containers. Transplant just before lights go out so plants have all night to recover from shock. See Transplanting in Chapter 7. Move lights up to 24 inches (61 cm) or more above plants for a day or two until transplant shock is over.

Growth Characteristics: During the third week of vegetative growth, plants will continue to develop strong root systems, and green leafy growth increases substantially.

Flush small plants with water before transplanting.

WEEK FOUR: First Week of Flowering

Light/dark: 12 hours day, 12 hours night
Light intensity: 400-watt lamp to 18 inches (45 cm) above flowering plants. Keep light at 24 inches (60 cm) if transplants look stressed.
Temperature: 75°F (24°C) day, 72°F (22°C) night
Humidity: 50% day, 50% night
pH: 6–6.5 pH soil, 5.5 pH hydroponics

Water: Plants need 25 ounces (75 cl) or more of water each week. Keep growing medium evenly moist so that roots stay wet but still have enough oxygen to take in nutrients. Continue to monitor water levels carefully to avoid overwatering and underwatering.

NOTE: Plants will need irrigation less often this week because they are in larger pots.

By the first week of flowering, plants should be about 14 inches (36 cm) tall.

Fertilizer: On Monday, switch to your favorite "bloom" nutrients with higher levels of potassium and phosphorus to stimulate bud growth; use per manufacturer's instructions. Add any additives suggested by the manufacturer. Pay special attention to the dosage calendar.

Growth Characteristics: The first week of flowering growth, plants will recover from transplanting and develop roots and green leafy growth. Stems start to elongate as plants start to prepare to flower.

CAUTION: Stress symptoms will be more evident now and appear in the form of slow growth, yellow and discolored foliage and burned leaf tips.

25 ounces

Diseases and pests may rear their ugly heads now. Inspect foliage and soil surface for signs of the two most common problems, fungus, and spider mites. See Chapter 12 Pests, Diseases, and Problems for control methods.

75 centileters

Switch to flowering nutrients.

Plants will recover from transplanting and develop roots and leafy growth.

Stems elongate as plants prepare to flower.

WEEK FIVE: Second Week of Flowering

Light/dark: 12 hours day, 12 hours night
Light intensity: 400-watt lamp to 18 inches (45 cm) above flowering plants
Temperature: 75°F (24°C) day, 72°F (22°C) night
Humidity: 50% day, 50% night
pH: 6–6.5 pH soil, 5.5 pH hydroponics

Water: Plants need one quart (1 L) or more of water each week. Avoid overwatering and underwatering.

The second week of flowering plants should be about 16 inches (41 cm) tall.

Fertilizer: Use your favorite "bloom" nutrients with higher levels of potassium and phosphorus to stimulate bud growth as per instructions. Add any additives suggested by the company, such as PK 13/14 below. P=potassium and K=phosphorus, 13/14 are the percentages of each.

NOTE: Monday add PK 13/14 or a similar product. On Friday add PK 13/14 again. This product is packed with more potassium (P) and phosphorus (K) for bigger, denser buds.

Growth Characteristics: The second week of flowering growth plants will continue to develop roots systems and green leafy growth increases. Fast-growing roots could start to poke out container drainage holes. Stems will elongate more this week.

NOTE: White, fuzzy, hairlike pistils sticking out of seed bracts should be visible on female plants.

CAUTION: Stress symptoms will be more evident now and appear in the form of slow growth, yellow and discolored foliage, and burned leaf tips. Control temperature, humidity, and moisture. Flush system and change nutrient solution.

PK 13/14

Remove all male plants as soon as they are identified.

Male plants will start to show first signs of flowering pollen sacks.

Diseases and pests will continue to become more of a problem if the room is not kept clean. Inspect foliage for signs of spider mites and other pests. Check soil surface for signs of fungus gnats.

Stems will elongate more this week

Weak underfertilized and underwatered plants like this are a target for pests and diseases.

WEEK SIX: Third Week of Flowering

The third week plants should be about 18 inches (45 cm) tall.

Light/dark: 12 hours day, 12 hours night
Light intensity: 400-watt lamp to 18 inches (45 cm) above flowering plants
Temperature: 75°F (24°C) day, 72°F (22°C) night
Humidity: 50% day, 50% night
pH: 6–6.5 pH soil, 5.5 pH hydroponics

Water: Plants need 1.5 quarts (1.5 L) or more of water a week. Keep growing medium moist. Avoid overwatering and underwatering. But if growing in soil, you may need to water every other day or when soil surface is dry about an inch (3 cm) deep.

Fertilizer: Use your favorite "bloom" nutrients with higher levels of potassium and phosphorus to stimulate bud growth as per instructions. Add any additives suggested by the company.

NOTE: Wednesday add PK 13/14 or a similar product.

Growth Characteristics: The third week of flowering growth plants will continue to develop roots and green leafy growth increases. Stem elongation continues but at a slower rate now. White fuzzy pistils on female plants will multiply and become more and more prominent. Remove plants with male flowers.

Weed out male plants!

Take clones now to pre-grow them for the next 8-week crop.

CAUTION: Stress symptoms will be more evident now and appear in the form of slow growth, yellow and discolored foliage, and burned leaf tips. Control stress by adjusting the environment to ideal conditions, and flush soil or change hydroponic nutrient solution in reservoir.

Diseases and pests will continue to become more of a problem if the room is not kept clean. Inspect foliage for spider mites. Check soil surface for signs of fungus gnats. See Chapter 12 for control measures.

White pistils appear now

Third week flowering California Orange.

White pistils continue to grow

This is what spider mite damage looks like on a leaf.

These plants will produce small buds because of heat and moisture stress.

WEEK SEVEN: Fourth Week of Flowering

During the fourth week of flowering, plants should be about 20 inches (51 cm) tall.

Light/dark: 12 hours day, 12 hours night
Light intensity: 400-watt lamp to 18 inches
(45 cm) above flowering plants
Temperature: 75°F (24°C) day, 72°F (22°C) night
Humidity: 50% day, 50% night
pH: 6–6.5 pH soil, 5.5 pH hydroponics

Water: Plants need 2 quarts (2 L) or more of water per week. Keep growing medium evenly moist. Monitor water levels carefully. Growing medium could start to dry out daily from now on.

On Friday flush plants with 3 times the volume of water as the volume of growing medium to wash out any built-up nitrogen in the growing medium. For example, flush a 3-gallon (11 L) container with 9 gallons (33 L) of water.

Fertilizer: Most manufacturers advise to increase fertilizer dosage this week. Use your favorite "bloom" nutrients with higher levels of potassium and phosphorus to stimulate bud growth as per instructions. Add any additives suggested by the company.

Growth Characteristics: During the fourth week of flowering, plants will continue to develop roots but much more energy is put into flower/bud formation. Elongation continues but at a very slow rate. Calyxes with pistils continue to develop and buds fill in and growing really starts to get exciting now!

Plant seeds for next crop.

Flush on Friday.

Flowering Afghani

Flowering Big Bud

You can also let runoff fill trays under plants if they can use all the water in less than 24 hours.

CAUTION: Stress symptoms will become apparent now and appear in the form of slow growth, yellow and discolored foliage, and burned leaf tips. Control stress by adjusting the environment to ideal conditions, and flush soil or change hydroponic nutrient solution in reservoir.

Diseases and pests will become problematic if the room is not kept clean. Inspect foliage for spider mites and other pests. Check soil surface for signs of fungus gnats. See Chapter 12 for control methods.

WEEK EIGHT: Fifth Week of Flowering

Light/dark: 12 hours day, 12 hours night
Light intensity: 400-watt lamp to 16–18 inches (40–45 cm) above flowering plants
Temperature: 75°F (24°C) day, 72°F (22°C) night
Humidity: 50% day, 50% night
pH: 6–6.5 pH soil, 5.5 pH hydroponics

Water: Plants need 2.5 quarts (2.5 L) or more of water a week. Keep growing medium evenly moist. Watch water levels carefully and avoid overwatering and underwatering.

Fertilizer: Use your favorite "bloom" nutrients with higher levels of potassium and phosphorus to stimulate bud growth as per instructions. Add any additives suggested by the company.

During the fifth week of flowering, plants should be about 22 inches (56 cm) tall.

Growth Characteristics: The fifth week of flowering, the plant will develop roots but much more energy is put into flower/bud formation. Stem elongation continues but at a very slow rate. Calyxes continue to develop and buds continue to fill in. Large older leaves may start to yellow now.

CAUTION: The unmistakable fragrance of fresh marijuana should start to become very prevalent this week. You will need to take measures to remove or filter it out with a carbon filter.

Take clones for next crop.

CAUTION: Stress symptoms will slow growth, yellow and discolor foliage, and burn leaf tips. See Chapter 12 for more information.

Diseases and pests will become problematic if the room is not kept clean. Inspect foliage for spider mites and other pests. See Chapter 12 for more details.

2.5 quart

2.5 liter

Change outside filter when it turns dark.

Nebula

Carbon filter

During the sixth week of flowering, plants should be about 22 inches (60 cm) tall.

2.5 quart

2.5 liter

WEEK NINE: Sixth Week of Flowering

Light/dark: 12 hours day, 12 hours night
Light intensity: 400-watt lamp to 16–18 inches (40–45 cm) above flowering plants
Temperature: 75°F (24°C) day, 72°F (22°C) night
Humidity: 50% day, 50% night
pH: 6–6.5 pH soil, 5.5 pH hydroponics

Water: Plants need 2.5 quarts (2.5 L) or more per week. Keep growing medium evenly moist. Monitor water levels carefully to avoid over-watering and underwatering.

Fertilizer: Use your favorite "bloom" nutrients with higher levels of potassium and phosphorus to stimulate bud growth as per instructions. Add any additives suggested by the company.

Growth Characteristics: This is the sixth week of flowering growth. Plants put much energy into flower/bud formation. Stem elongation continues but very, very slowly. Calyxes with white fuzzy pistils continue to develop, and buds start to put on weight. Larger leaves continue to yellow and discolor.

Remove bottom branches that impair air circulation between plants to guard against fungus.

CAUTION: Stress will slow growth, yellow and discolor foliage, and burn leaf tips.

CAUTION: The unmistakable fragrance of fresh marijuana will be more and more dominant this week. You must remove or filter it out before expelling outdoors.

Diseases and pests will become problematic if the room is not kept clean. Inspect foliage for spider mites and other pests and diseases. Check soil surface for signs of fungus gnats. See Chapter 12 for control methods.

Lavender

Watch out for spider mites!

If bud mold *(botrytis)* appears in buds, remove it immediately and wash cutting tools in alcohol to sterilize.

WEEK TEN: Seventh Week of Flowering

Light/dark: 12 hours day, 12 hours night
Light intensity: 400-watt lamp to 16–18 inches (40–45 cm) above flowering plants.
Temperature: 75°F (24°C) day, 72°F (22°C) night
Humidity: 50% day, 50% night
pH: 6–6.5 pH soil, 5.5 pH hydroponics

Water: Plants need 2.5 quarts (2.5 L) or more of water a week. Keep growing medium evenly moist. Watch water levels carefully to avoid overwatering and underwatering.

Fertilizer: Use your favorite "bloom" nutrients with higher levels of potassium and phosphorus to stimulate bud growth as per instructions. Add any additives suggested by the company.

During the seventh week of flowering, plants should be about 24 inches (61cm) tall.

Growth Characteristics: During the seventh week of flowering growth, plants put energy into flower/bud formation. Stem elongation virtually stops. Calyxes continue to develop and buds really pack on weight; buds start to get hard and plump! Large leaves continue to yellow and discolor. Leaves around buds may show burned tips and become brittle, especially if given high doses of fertilizer.

Stress will slow growth, yellow and discolor foliage, and burn leaf tips.

CAUTION: The fragrance of fresh marijuana will be very strong this week if growing potent strains. Take measures to remove or filter it out. Check filter for efficiency.

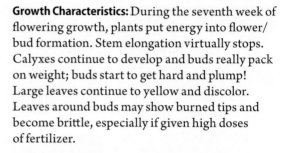

Diseases and pests will continue if the room is not kept clean. Inspect foliage for spider mites and other pests and diseases. Check soil surface for signs of fungus gnats. Check for bud mold (*botrytis*) See Chapter 12 for control methods

NOTE: Stop all spraying this week.

Lightly squeeze buds to feel if they are thick and resinous.

WEEK ELEVEN: Eighth Week of Flowering

Light/dark: 12 hours day, 12 hours night
Light intensity: 400-watt lamp to 16–18 inches
    (40–45 cm) above flowering plants.
Temperature: 75°F (24°C) day, 72°F (22°C) night
Humidity: 50% day, 50% night
pH: 6–6.5 pH soil, 5.5 pH hydroponics

Water: Plants need progressively more water, 2.5 quarts (2.5 L) or more per week. Stop watering 3 days before harvest to start removing water from growing medium, and plants will dry faster.

On Monday flush plants with 3 times the volume of water as the volume of growing medium to wash out any built-up nitrogen in the growing medium. For example, flush a 1-gallon (4 L) container with 3 gallons (12 L) of water. You might want to use a "clearing agent" such as Final Flush.

During the eighth week of flowering plants should be about 24 inches (61 cm) tall.

Fertilizer: Stop fertilizing this week and apply plain water to wash out built-up fertilizer from growing medium. Some growers stop fertilizing 10 days before harvest to allow plants to use all the fertilizer so that buds, when smoked, do not taste like fertilizer.

Growth Characteristics: This is harvest week! During the eighth week of flowering plants will continue to develop roots but much more energy is put into flower/bud formation. Calyxes with pistils continue to develop, and buds put on more and more weight until harvest. Large leaves will be yellow, and smaller leaves could be discolored with dark tips.

CAUTION: Stress symptoms will become very apparent now, appearing in the form of slow growth, yellow and discolored foliage, and burned leaf tips.

Diseases and pests: Cut out any bud mold you find. Nothing can be done for latent spider mites and other pests. They will bunch up at the top of buds or escape out the end of the drying line.

CAUTION: The fragrance of fresh marijuana will be the strongest this week if growing potent strains. Take measures to remove or filter out fragrance.

Hash plant

AK47

Brainwarp

Grapefruit Haze, dry

Romulan

Reclining Buddha

Burmese #1

Purple Deisel

Giant AK47 bud

WEEK TWELVE: Drying

Once harvested, the crop must be dried. Manicure buds and hang them on lines or set on screens to dry. Store buds in airtight containers to preserve freshness. See Chapter 8: Harvesting for more information.

Hang buds in a closet or set buds on screens to dry.

The payoff for all the hard work is an abundant harvest!

Enclosed drying screens with a small vent fan.

CHAPTER 11

Fifty-four Different Grow Rooms

INTRODUCTION

This grow room tour is simple and easy. Just take a look at the photos and read the captions. Study the photos because there are many details that are not pointed out in the text. This section starts with cloning rooms then progresses to small rooms and larger rooms. At the end you will find commercial grow closets that will show you how successful you can be!

Ten Clone Rooms

Clone rooms come in all shapes and sizes. You will need a mother plant or mother plants to provide you with clones. Keep the mother plants as healthy as possible so that they will provide strong healthy clones. Sick pest- and disease-infested mothers yield sick pest- and disease-infested clones!

This short section shows you a few mothers and clone-room setups that we could not fit anywhere else in the book!

1 This great-looking basement mother room is illuminated with a single 600-watt HP sodium lamp mounted on a light track attached to floor joists that are painted white. The productive mothers get plenty of air circulation provided by four oscillating circulation fans. The airflow is such that exhaust air escapes from the room between floor joists. A flexible intake duct, located upper right, feeds fresh air directly into the garden. The fresh air is pushed down toward plants with the oscillating circulation fan. The room is lined with white Visqueen plastic, and mothers are growing in 5-gallon (20 L) containers of their special soil mix. These mothers produce hundreds of clones every few weeks and have a life span of about six months.

2 Keep your clones in an environment with plenty of humidity for the first few days to reduce stress after the branch tip has been cut from the mother. This small humidifier is filled with water and vapor soon billows out the front to elevate relative humidity in the microclimate around clones. This cloning chamber is lit with fixtures that hold two 55-watt CFL lamps. More mother plants are located to the right and in the background.

3 This mass of clones and seedlings is being grown to move outdoors. The garden is below a 400-watt metal halide lamp that is suspended from the ceiling in a corner of a room. Some plants have been moved into larger containers and are big enough to move outdoors. They will be acclimated (hardened-off) for a week to the harsher outdoor climate before transplanting. The smaller plants will be potted up into larger containers and moved outdoors or into the flowering room in about a month. The small envelopes contain beneficial insects.

4 Starting a grow room is as easy as clearing out a cabinet, setting up a light, and moving in a crop of clones or seedlings. Of course, this new grow room will need a vent fan and a circulation fan. The grower will also paint the interior white and line the bottom with plastic to protect the wood and contain irrigation runoff. Once clones are transplanted into larger containers, they will be set up on blocks so they are closer to the 110-watt CFL fixture.

5 This simple-to-set-up grow cabinet is placed on a couple of shelves purchased at a building supply store. The mother plants are positioned above and the clones below. There is no front door, which diminishes the need for ventilation. The plants are growing relatively slowly and do not need much water or fertilizer to meet their needs. It is very easy to overwater plants that are growing slowly. You can also augment light plants receive by moving them outdoors or under an HID lamp for a few hours whenever possible.

6 This cloning room is amazing! Humidity is maintained at around 70 percent and the temperature at about 70°F (20°C) both day and night. As you can see, the clones appear to like it! The 1000-watt metal halide above the big bed on the right illuminates hundreds of clones and is much less hassle to set up and use than a bunch of fluorescent tubes or CFL fixtures. The 1000-watt HID is about 4.5 feet (135 cm) above the rooting clones. The clones on the lower left are new and need less light for a few days. The new clones will be moved to the big table when those rooted clones are moved to the flowering room. The grower sticks five or six stems in four-inch rockwool cubes and keeps them in plastic trays that are easy to handle.

7 Sixteen Standard T-12 Cool White fluorescent tubes (640 watts) illuminate these clones that are ready to transplant. Clones are rooted in flats of Grodan rockwool. With more than 100 individual one-inch cubes per flat and abundant light, clones are ready to transplant after 14 days of rooting. K from Trichome Technologies settled on Vita-Grow Rooting Compound (hormone) after trying a myriad of other brands. Roots are not visible because they grow out the bottom of cubes and as you can see foliage is already growing toward the lights.

A clear dome covers clones to maintain humidity at 80 percent. Humidity decreases to 60 percent when domes are removed to harden-off clones for transplanting. The growers keep the temperature at 80°F (26.5°C) both day and night.

8 Both clones and seedlings are growing in this garden. The grower roots the clones and seedlings. Then he moves them to the next tray to resume vegetative growth. Once plants have grown for three weeks in the vegetative growth stage, they are ready to move into the flowering room.

9 This clone setup is about as simple as you can get. The grower hung two 40-watt fluorescents over a tray of clones covered with a humidity dome. Every day the grower removes the dome to check moisture content and the health of clones.

10 This is one of my favorite clone room photos. You can see the recently rooted clones have been transplanted into larger containers. Pots of clones are moved for progressively more and brighter light. In the beginning, clones and seedlings need little light. As they grow they use more light.

Twenty-two Small Grow Rooms

1 This small, white closet was very easy to set up, and it took only about four hours. The budding clones are growing in one-gallon containers of soilless mix and sitting in 10 × 20-inch (25 × 50 cm) trays lined with a plastic grate to facilitate drainage. Flypaper is stretched across the back of the room to monitor flying insect populations.

A small 250-watt HP sodium illuminates this 2 × 2-foot (60 × 60 cm) garden. The grower could have waited until plants were a little taller before inducing flowering to increase yield.

Here is a close-up of the buds in the garden at left a couple of weeks later. The single 600-watt HP sodium light provides more than enough light to harvest a heavy crop in this 40 × 40-inch (1 x 1 m) garden.

2 This small grow room was set up in the corner of a room that is lined with white Visqueen to protect the walls and reflect light. Rockwool blocks are set on rockwool slabs covered with black plastic, which inhibits algae growth.

3 This top-feed hydroponic garden under self-vented 400-watt HP sodium is set up in a utility room. The other things stored in the room make it difficult to maintain the garden, and the walls provide very little reflection.

4 Set hydroponic and soil gardens up on a bed 18–24 inches (45–60 cm) so that gravity can carry irrigated nutrient solution back to the nutrient tank below. The shadow on the wall tells you the light hood needs to be adjusted so that plants receive more even lighting.

5 The clones in this hydroponic garden are just starting to grow. They were transplanted too early, before the root systems had properly developed, a mistake that cost the grower two full weeks of slow growth. Regardless of the amount of money spent on grow gear, mistakes like this still slow progress.

6 We call it Mecalux in Spain (see below), the industrial metal shelving which frames this 40-inch-square (1 × 1 m) garden. These stressed-out females suspended by plant yo-yos are growing on a shelf that is four feet (1.2 m) from the ground. The lower half of the room could serve as a clone room or be used to store growing supplies.

7 Mother plants are growing under a single 400-watt metal halide lamp in eight-gallon (30 L) pots of soilless mix. Notice how light shines in a hot spot directly below the bulb. Bending plants will disperse light so that all plants receive more overall light.

8 Check out the roots on this hydroponically grown plant! This is an excellent example of a strong, healthy root system. The grower glued Styrofoam panels to the far wall; these panels insulate against hot and cold temperatures and reflect light, too.

9 Suspending a fan from the shroud near the grow room doorway with lightweight rope or bungee cords is a temporary and unsafe option. Serious growers mount the fan firmly on a wall or shelf.

10 Bathtubs can make good grow spaces. Drainage is not a problem and the walls are waterproof. Make sure the lamp and all other electrical appliances are plugged into a ground fault interrupt (GFI) outlet. But most growers use bathtubs to leach (flush) toxic fertilizer salts from soil. Flushing the growing medium every 30 days will avert many possible problems.

11 This photo shows a bright hot spot concentrated in the center of the garden while less light reaches the perimeter of the bed, which is significantly darker. Much light is also shining off to the side of the garden, wasted in space. Simply by turning the lamp 90 degrees, the entire garden would receive considerably more light.

12 This series of five photos of the same garden shows two different crops. The first crop suffered much fertilizer, temperature, and humidity stress. The grower also got a little carried away removing leaves. In fact, I am amazed the garden turned out so well afterward.

This photo of the same garden was taken a week before harvest. The flowering females received consistent care. Buds look pretty good considering how sickly the scrawny plants looked a few weeks before.

By the second attempt, the grower had more experience and was able to keep the fertilizer, temperature, and humidity under control. You can tell this crop will grow much better than the last one. Plants look much healthier.

The profile of this hydroponic garden is much greener than the first. At the top you can see the air vent and a little bit of the 400-watt HP sodium dangling above the garden.

A few weeks later, the same plants are flowering and producing respectable buds. This short series of photos shows how just a little tender loving care can make all the difference at harvest time!

14 This grow room is framed with 2 × 4-inch (5 × 10 cm) boards and covered with white Visqueen plastic. Velcro at the top and bottom of the doorway holds the plastic in place. A bit of reflective Mylar helps direct light too. The 400-watt HP sodium lamp provides all the light necessary to harvest a nice crop of buds from the 40-inch-square (1 × 1 m) grow room. The calendar attached to the outside wall helps the grower schedule regular fertilization and maintenance.

13 Plants are set up on buckets and a board, which form a growing platform and work/smoking bench. The 40-inch-square (1 × 1 m) drain table contains the three-gallon (11 L) pots full of soilless mix. A small extraction vent fan in the upper left-hand corner moves old, stale air out of the room. A circulation fan shroud on the right is visible. The leggy, stressed plants were induced to flower too late, when about 24 inches (60 cm) tall.

15 Section off a cubicle in an unused portion of the garage, basement, or spare room. Line the walls with Mylar and the floor with plastic. Hang a 400-watt metal halide, plop in some clones, and you have a grow room!

17 These clones (above) have been moved into a small grow room and will be transplanted into two-gallon (7.5 L) containers. A few days after transplanting, the grower will change the fixture from the current 110-watt CFL setup to a 400-watt HP sodium lamp to illuminate this 2.5 × 3-foot (75 × 90 cm) closet garden.

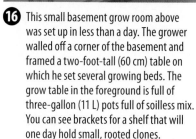

16 This small basement grow room above was set up in less than a day. The grower walled off a corner of the basement and framed a two-foot-tall (60 cm) table on which he set several growing beds. The grow table in the foreground is full of three-gallon (11 L) pots full of soilless mix. You can see brackets for a shelf that will one day hold small, rooted clones.

18 Haze-dominant *sativa* strains like these at right take longer to flower, and central buds often spike to make even lighting in small and large rooms alike a challenge. A simple solution to unwieldy growth is to train plants by tying branches to a trellis, starting in the vegetative growth stage. Make trellises from wood, wire, or my favorite—plastic netting.

19
20 Even small, one-light rooms (above and right) need adequate ventilation and a good activated charcoal filter to ensure no unwanted fragrances leave the grow space. Remember, it is much easier to set up an air filter than it is to explain to your landlord or the cops why you did not!

21 Commercial grow closets make setting up a grow room quick and easy. More and more growers are opting for prefabricated grow closets so they can concentrate on growing plants rather than grow room construction and fiddling with all the details in order to get plants to produce well. See Commercial Grow Closets in this chapter.

22 The plants in this little two-light room are set up on a drainage table with a reservoir below to catch runoff nutrient solution. Plants have plenty of space to grow and all the air circulation and ventilation they need.

Twenty-two Large Grow Rooms

1 Here are two photos of a garden. The first photo was taken in the vegetative growth stage when the plants were about a foot (30 cm) tall, just before they were induced to flower. The garden is in the corner of a spare bedroom and illuminated by two 400-watt metal halide lamps. Clones were transplanted into three-gallon (11 L) containers of soilless mix. Note the small envelopes of beneficial insects clipped to the containers on the lower left.

Here is the same garden after a few weeks of flowering. The grower changed lamps to 400-watt HP sodiums and moved one of the circulation fans up higher so that it would not blow directly on plants, which would have dried them out.

2 The dense foliage in this garden lit with six 600-watt HP sodium lamps shows some of the problems confronted by success! The foliage is so dense that it is difficult to get air to circulate between plants. The photo has a monochromatic yellow tint from the dominant HP sodium light. The grower uses the single green incandescent lightbulb (center top) to turn on in emergencies in case he has to work in the garden during the dark period while plants are flowering.

3 A web of drip emitters delivers nutrient solution to this hydroponic rockwool garden. Irrigating such a garden by hand would surely break stems and destroy foliage. Note that this modular trough hydroponic garden is set up on sawhorses. The troughs nest inside one another and the sawhorses collapse, making the garden quick to assemble, disassemble, and stow in a small space.

4 This three-light garden has plenty of room to grow. The grower blacked out the window, hung the lights, set up a couple of circulation fans, and moved rooted clones into the garden. He could have covered the parquet floor with plastic to save it from water damage. The only ventilation is provided by a circulation fan stationed in front of an open door.

Here is the same room a few weeks later, in full bloom. Harvest time is near! Obviously, the ventilation system was able to supply enough air to grow a healthy harvest. Fortunately, fragrance was not an issue!

5 Check out all the appliances in this room—circulation fans, air conditioner, thermometers/hygrometers on three levels, hydroponic system, two 400-watt lamps (heat from which is vented separately), and, of course, crystal balls and a sound system! The grower turns a crop every eight weeks. You do not have to go to these ends to grow a great crop, but it will give you exacting control.

6 Three lamps on retractable tethers illuminate this garden that is easy-to-access with a wheelchair. Most of the growing beds are set up on large casters so they can be moved and maintained easily. The white bucket under the beige grow table catches runoff irrigation water.

7 Build a free-standing grow table/light stand like this one and leave no traces of construction. The growing table is set up on small sawhorses a 2 × 4-inch (5 × 10 cm) post in the center of each end of the table with a 2 × 4 board (5 × 10 cm) between serves as a light stand. Corner posts on the table serve as anchors for strings to contain plants. The floor is covered with heavy duty plastic to save the hardwood from damage.

Here is the same grow table from a different camera angle. As you can see, plants don't mind growing in a quick-to-set-up simple garden that leaves no traces!

8 With a couple of 400-watt lamps, you can grow consecutive crops very easily. The crop on the right is four weeks older than the upcoming crop on the left. Two HP sodium lamps give this grower the flexibility of growing tall *sativa*-dominant plants on the right and short *indica*-dominant plants on the left. The *indica* strains have a much lower profile, making it easier to keep the lamp closer to the canopy.

9 This grower removed the bottom leaves on these plants because they were small and yellow due to lack of light. Removing lower foliage allows for more ventilation between plants and sends all growing energy to upper branches.

10 In this before and after photo sequence we see a crop of clones growing in the corner of a room under two HID lamps. The floor is lined with plastic to contain runoff water, and the window is blacked out.

NOTE: the exterior of the window is covered with a roll-down shutter identical to all the other shutters on the house, and does not raise any suspicions.

Here is the same garden a few weeks later in full bloom. The yellow tint is from the two 400-watt HP sodium lamps. The grower keeps the maximum/minimum thermometer/hygrometer just above the canopy of the garden to make sure the buds do not burn from intense light.

This photo was taken a few days before harvest.

11 This rockwool hydroponic trough garden is a few weeks from harvest. It was set up in the corner of the room—beginning to end—in just four hours. The grower taped white plastic Visqueen to the wall and suspended a lamp from a hook in the ceiling before setting up the hydroponic garden on collapsible sawhorses. Each trough is drained individually by inverting the drain "elles" that also serve to maintain the level of nutrient solution.

This photo, snapped the day of harvest, shows that the irrigation manifold is attached to the wall. Once pumped up to the large tube, the nutrient solution will flow evenly down the spaghetti tubes to plants. I like this setup because it is efficient as well as easy to monitor and control.

12 Located in an old garage and planted in an "L" shape, this four-light 600-watt HP sodium garden is sitting on a two-foot-tall bed to allow for drainage and convenient maintenance. The raised bed also keeps plants off the cold concrete floor, which elevates soil temperature and makes it easier to regulate.

13 This hydroponic coco slab grow room is anything but anarchistic, as the flag might lead you to believe. It is set up with order and precision. The retractable hangers make adjusting lamp height simple and easy.

Well-rooted clones are transplanted into bottomless containers full of coco peat, and then set on slabs of Canna Coco. Adjustable-flow nozzles meter the exact dose of nutrient solution to individual plants.

14 Clones on the lower right receive extra light when the flowering lamps are on, and are covered to prevent light leaks when the flowering lamps are off. Insulated ducting dampens noise and maintains intake air temperature. Two oscillating circulation fans keep the air stirred up in this half of the room. A heat-generating ballast is mounted on the wall in the upper left corner of the room to keep hot air high in the room.

An oscillating circulation fan also blows on the other half of the same flowering room. Insulated extraction ducting attached to a charcoal filter dampens vibrations and noise.

15 Remodeled Conex transportation containers make excellent grow rooms. Since they are portable, containers do not need a special building permit to site. Insulated aluminum containers that were used to transport cold perishable merchandise are favored over uninsulated steel ones that are also susceptible to rust. This steel container has the special feature of a drain down one side which facilitates drainage and maintenance. See www.portablecontainerservices.com for more information on Conex containers.

16 The walls of this bedroom are covered with white Visqueen plastic to protect walls and reflect light. Intake air is supplied via several runs of flexible ducting. Lights are suspended from 1 × 2-inch (3 × 5 cm) boards. NOTE: lamps are numbered to correspond with a number on remote ballasts. Numbering ballasts that go with lamps will facilitate troubleshooting electrical problems.

17 This overhead shot of a precision hydroponic garden from Trichome Technologies in California supplies one of the many medical dispensaries with top-quality cannabis. Custom-made tables support 192 clones planted in 3-inch (8 cm) Grodan cubes planted on 12-inch (30 cm) centers in a total grow bed space of 88 square feet (8 m²). K uses General Hydroponics Flora Series fertilizer in the automated irrigation system that applies nutrient solution two minutes six times daily.

The garden is illuminated with three alternating 1000-watt metal halide and three HP sodium 1000-watt lamps. Lights are kept 24 inches (60 cm) above the garden canopy during vegetative growth and 36 inches (90 cm) above plants during flowering. K keeps the lights further away during flowering to lower heat levels on foliage that appears to evaporate some of the resin.

Buds are so big and heavy that each plant is supported by 36-inch (90 cm) nursery stakes placed in every 6-inch (15 cm) (0.75-gallon [3.3 L]) container. This crop is in the same space as the above garden but planted in soilless mix. Oddly enough, plants in soilless mix and rockwool produce about the same volume of buds, but K prefers to work with 3-inch (8 cm) Grodan cubes because they are easier to use and require less work to set up. Once used, cubes are collected and compacted in a trash compacter, which makes a nice inconspicuous package to toss out.

K finds that soil is more complex to use—messy, and much more time consuming. Soil must also be watered by hand because each of the 11 strains growing in the photo requires a little different care. When watering by hand it is easy to miss a pot or overwater containers.

Here is the soil mix he uses:

0.3 Super Soil from Home Depot

0.3 vermiculite

0.3 perlite

0.25 teaspoon of water-retaining crystals per 0.75-gallon (0.3 L) pot to give buffer

K trims the stems of clones up from the bottom two days after going into the flowering room. He removes any leaves or those that receive minimal light. After testing plants with bottom foliage stripped and others with full foliage he found that both plants produce the same amount at harvest, but plants with stripped stems develop bigger thicker buds that are much easier to harvest and manicure. Un-stripped plants tend to have more wispy buds that are difficult to manicure.

18 This medicinal garden located in Oaksterdam (aka Oakland), California, supplies pharmaceutical-grade cannabis to local dispensaries. Note how the shadow on the far wall comes down to the top of the canopy of plants, which denotes even distribution of light over plants. The fans next to the lamps blow hot air generated by lamps down toward plants.

Nutrient solution is pumped from reservoirs in foreground and delivered to plants via a hose and water wand. A roll-up wheel keeps heavy water-laden hose off the floor.

The white signs on the pots read "Juries cannot be prosecuted for their verdicts."

A fire extinguisher is important in all grow rooms. Make sure to purchase a fire extinguisher that is rated for class A, B, and C fires for your grow room.

- **Class A** extinguishes fires fueled by wood, paper, cloth, rubber, and most plastics.
- **Class B** extinguishes flammable liquids such as gasoline, oil, and grease.
- **Class C** is for wiring, appliance, and electrical fires.

19 The complex tangle of ducting directs hot air generated by lamps out of this grow room. Every time ducting turns corners, air-movement efficiency is impaired. Keep the ducting as straight as possible to get the most from the extraction fan and ducting setup. See Air Ducting in Chapter 9: Grow Gear for more information.

The grower measures the temperature and humidity at the base of plants and between buds and lamps. An automatic controller (blue meter in back of garden) keeps the atmosphere and nutrient solution constantly regulated in this hydroponic system filled with Hydroton, expanded clay pellets.

20 The ballast sitting on a plastic-covered chair at lower right is a fire disaster waiting to happen. The air ventilation ducting goes around so many corners that efficiency is cut my nearly 90 percent. Leggy budded plants are so weak that they fall on one another and cut light to one another. Although difficult to see in the intertwined foliage, drip emitters are plugged and deliver nutrient solution to about half the plants.

21 Two identical grow beds are located in frames of 1 × 3-inch (3 × 8 cm) boards covered with plastic to protect the carpet. Pots sit up on a plastic grate to keep roots from drowning in runoff water. The lights are vented individually from the room. The brown square in the back of the bedroom is the fresh air vent. The room is vented into a closed-off end of the room where odor is filtered and later extracted outdoors.

22 Here are two photos from a high-tech, medicinal rockwool/Hydroton hydroponic garden in Oakland, California. The piece of paper tacked to the overhead frame indicates technical growth data about the strain being grown. The number "12" next to the paper designates the bed number. Note that each container is labeled with the strain being grown. Such precise control helps the head grower track the progress of each and every plant in this garden.

A close-up of another bed in the garden shows two 600-watt lamps over a 4 × 8-foot (1.2 × 2.4 m) garden packed with high-quality budded plants. Note that plenty of light is available for plants to grow big, dense buds. Foliage is trimmed from lower stems to allow for air circulation between plants.

Four Commercial Grow Closets

When purchasing a commercial grow closet, consider the following:

- **Price:** Does it fit within your budget?
- **Completeness:** Does it contain everything you need to start growing, or will you need to buy extra stuff now and later?
- **Size:** How big is it? Will it fit in your allotted space?
- **Location:** Where will you set it up? Do you have an outlet for the exhaust/extraction fan? Do you have electrical outlets?
- **Self-contained:** Does it stand alone or does it need support such as an exterior reservoir?
- **Discreet:** Can you put it in a corner of your home? What will it look like to visitors?
- **Fragrance:** Does it have a carbon filter?
- **Noise:** How much noise will it make? Are the walls insulated against noise? How quiet (decibel rating) are the fans?
- **Electrical use:** How much electricity (watts and amperes) will it use?
- **Lights:** How many and what wattage are the lights? Will they create too much heat for your specific growing situation?

- **Temperature and humidity:** How are temperature and humidity measured and controlled?
- **Hydroponic or soil system:** Is the growing system fail-safe even for beginners? How big is the reservoir, and how often should it be refilled?
- **Technical support:** Can you call the supplier or manufacturer for answers to your questions? How stable is the manufacturer? How long have they been in business?
- **Convenience:** How long can you leave it without checking on it?

Check the following web sites and compare the features of different models of grow closets. At publication this list was fairly complete. Search www.google.com for more sites and information.

www.bcnorthernlights.com
www.globalhydro.net
www.the-homebox.net
www.growcabinets.co.uk
www.growboxbreda.nl
www.g-tools.nl
www.hi-techgrowsystems.com
www.homegrown-hydroponics.com
www.hydroasis.com
www.igrow.nl
www.quickgrow.com

1 The self-sufficient BC Northern Lights BloomBox: 110-volt 15-ampere plug-in, add seeds and nutrients, and turn it on. The grow closet measures 54 × 51 × 28 inches (140 × 130 × 70 cm). Controlled by GroSmart computer technology, the unit is preprogrammed to control water, CO_2, light and air circulation, and exhaust.

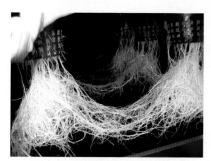

A hydroponic system supported by a space-saving aerated reservoir feeds plants located in net pots.

Two 430-watt HP sodium air-cooled fixtures are designed to grow 18 flowering plants to harvest. A coco carbon filter absorbs pungent pot odors before expelling air. Comes complete with a simple grow manual and unlimited toll-free technical support. Check their site, www. bcnorthernlights.com, for more information.

2 The 70 × 60 × 30-inch (176 × 154 × 78 cm) G-Kit from G-Tools is constructed with lightweight aluminum and PVC panels. The extraction fans and carbon filters keep this plug-and-play grow closet cool, odor-free, and light-tight.

No tools are required to set up this completely automated grow closet. Good grow instructions, including a manual, are supplied with the G-Kit.

You can also choose to put the lights in the middle of the unit and run the hydroponic beds alongside the walls.

3 Assemble the 58 × 44 × 80-inch (146.5 × 112 × 203 cm) iGrow PVC cabinet with a simple "click" system. Light generated by two 600-watt lamps does not escape from the single flowering room.

The hydroponic Mapito system also has an exterior 26-gallon (100 L) reservoir. The constant-feed aerated system ensures plants constant feeding.

Two humming ceiling-mounted extractor fans attached to carbon filters are regulated by a thermostat to maintain proper temperatures and keep fragrances from escaping.

The HomeBox is set up to mount the fan and carbon air filter. it is easy to mount the heavy filter and fan with the straps provided.

4 There is an excellent QuickTime movie about setting up a HOMEbox at http://www.homebox.net/dhtml/downloads.php. Or Just type "Homebox Grow" into www.google.com and you will find a screen full of HOMEbox distributors.

Installing the filter and attached fan as well as directing the ducting outside the room takes just a few minutes.

This setup keeps the lamp cool as well as the room. The lamp is raised and lowered with retractable cords.

CHAPTER 12

Pests, Diseases, and Problems

INTRODUCTION

Cleanliness is the secret to disease and pest prevention. Keep floor, ground, and substrate surface clean. Dirty tools often carry microscopic pests and diseases. Wearing clean clothes and using clean tools will reduce problems. A separate set of indoor tools is easy to keep clean.

Wash your hands if you touch diseased plants. Pay attention to simple hygiene. Do not work in the dirty outdoor garden and then visit the indoor garden. Even walking across a lawn or brushing up against outdoor plants could carry pests and diseases to your indoor garden. Stay away from dogs, cats, and other pets that have been outdoors, and don't let them in the garden. Houseplants can also help spread pests and disease.

Keep all debris off the floor. Clean the garden area regularly.

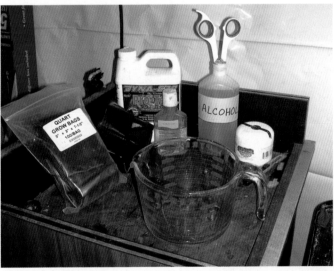

Dip tools in alcohol to disinfect.

	HUMIDITY DAY	**HUMIDITY NIGHT**	**TEMP DAY**	**TEMP NIGHT**
Seedlings	60%	55%–60%	75°F (24°C)	75°F (24°C)
Clones	100%–70%	100%–70%	75°F (24°C)	75°F (24°C)
Vegetative	60%	50%–60%	75°F (24°C)	70°F (21°C)
Flowering	50%	50%	75°F (24°C)	70°F (21°C)

Wash your hands to avoid transmitting insects and diseases from other plants.

Grow insect- and fungus-resistant strains like Power Plant and keep the garden strong and healthy. Keep air well-circulated and fresh. Keep humidity around 50 percent and maintain the temperature at about 75°F (24°C) during the day and about 5°F (3°C) cooler at night.

Keep the temperature and humidity at the proper levels to avoid cultural, pest, and disease problems.

Make sure there is plenty of ventilation and air circulation.

Misdiagnosed Disorders

Many indoor garden problems are misdiagnosed as a lack or excess of fertilizer. Often, disease and insects cause such problems. Other times, problems are caused by an imbalanced growing medium or water pH. Keep the pH from 5.5–6.5, in hydroponics, and 6–6.5 in soil gardens to allow nutrients to be chemically available.

Temperature and humidity also influence growth. Keep them in the range of 70°–75°F (21°–24°C) day and about 65°–70°F (18°–21°C) night and keep humidity 55–65 percent vegetative room and 50 percent flowering room.

Excess sodium (more than 50 ppm) in the water supply restricts water and nutrients from being absorbed by the roots.

Do not confuse nutrient deficiencies or toxicities with insect and disease damage or poor cultural practices.

Avoid most common ailments by keeping temperature, humidity, and light at the proper levels. Use clean water, the proper complete nutrient solution, maintain EC and pH at the correct proportions, and change and flush the system with fresh nutrient solution every week if necessary.

DAMAGE FROM CULTURAL PRACTICES	
CULTURAL PRACTICE	SYMPTOM
Lack of ventilation to the plant	slow growth and curled-down leaves
Lack of light	slow, spindly growth and stretching between internodes
Excessive humidity	slow growth and curled-down leaves
Not enough humidity	seldom a problem and plants use more water
Temperature too high	slow growth and drooping leaves
Temperature too low	slow growth, purpling, and no flowers
Spray application damage	burned spots
Ozone damage	burned patches on leaves
Overwatering	slow growth, disease and nutrient deficiencies
Underwatering	wilting, slow growth, disease and nutrient deficiencies
Light burn	burned patches on leaves
Indoor air pollution	slow growth and sickly appearance

Pests and Diseases

This section covers the most common pests and diseases that attack plants in a grow room. The descriptions and methods of control are simple and straightforward. If you have more questions about pests and diseases not answered in this book, please consult *Marijuana Horticulture: The Indoor/Outdoor Medical Grower's Bible*, which covers in much more detail solutions to controlling just about any pest and disease that attacks cannabis.

Spider Mites

Spider mites are common indoors. Find spider mites on leaf undersides, sucking plant fluids. They look like tiny specks and cause yellowish-white spots on the tops of leaves. If infested, spider webs may be seen when misted with water. A 10X–30X magnifying glass helps to identify the yellow, white, two-spotted, brown, or red mites and their translucent eggs.

Control spider mites by:
- Cleaning up regularly
- Raising humidity and lowering temperature
- Smearing Tanglefoot™ around the pot lip and stems
- Dipping small plants and spraying large ones with pyrethrum or neem oil
- Introducing predatory mites

Stipples caused by mites.

Mites on leaf underside.

Spider mite infestation!

Whiteflies

Whiteflies flutter from under leaves when disturbed. They look like a small, white moth about one millimeter long. Adults have wings. Eggs are also found on leaf undersides. Whiteflies cause whitish speckles, stipples, on the tops of leaves.

Attract and kill adults with bright yellow sticky traps that are placed among plants. The wasp *Encarsia formosa* is the most effective whitefly parasite. Kill with insecticidal soap or pyrethrum applied at five- to ten-day intervals.

Whiteflies are between yellowish aphids. The dark spots are honeydew that has attracted mold.

Fungus Gnats

Dark specks are fungus gnats. Larvae grow four
to five millimeters long with translucent bodies
and black heads. Winged adults are gray to black
with long legs. Pests infest growing mediums and
roots, eating and scarring roots. Plants loose
vigor, foliage pales, and wounds invite disease.

Control with Vectobac®, Gnatrol® and *Bt-i*.
Use neem or insecticidal soap as a soil drench.
Predatory soil mites are also available.

Gray Mold *(Botrytis)*

Gray mold (aka bud mold) flourishes in moist,
temperate climates and can be fatal. *Botrytis*
appears hairlike, similar to laundry lint, and later
turns slimy but can appear as dark, brownish
spots on stems and flowers in arid climates. It
attacks stems, leaves, and seeds, and can cause
damping-off.

Once it starts, gray mold is fatal. If on buds,
cut buds off one inch (3 cm) below infestation.
Prevent gray mold by increasing air circulation
and ventilation. Use fresh, clean growing
medium. Remove infected foliage with alcohol-
sterilized pruners, and destroy it. Wash your
hands and tools.

Gray mold on bud   *Botrytis* damage   This bud is gone!

Rotten stem

Damaged stem and roots

Damping-off

Damping-off is fatal. It prevents sprouted seeds from emerging. Seedlings and cuttings rot at the soil line. Foliage in older plants yellows and stems rot. First, the stem loses girth at the soil line, grows dark, and finally falls over.

Once it starts, damping-off is fatal. Avoid by controlling growing-medium moisture. Dust seeds with fungicide.

Damping-off rots seedlings and cuttings at the soil line.

Green algae grow in light and nutrient-rich environments. Avoid algae by covering growing mediums.

Green Algae

Slimy, green algae need nutrients, light, and a moist surface to grow. Algae grow on moist rockwool and other moist-growing mediums exposed to light. Algae cause little damage, but attract fungus gnats and other pests and diseases.

Prevent by covering moist-growing mediums to exclude light. Control by adding an algaecide to the nutrient solution.

Downy Mildew

Sometimes called "false mildew," downy mildew affects vegetative and flowering plants. It appears as whitish-yellow spots on top of leaves, creating pale patches. Grayish mycelium spawn is on leaf under-sides, opposite the pale patches.

Control with cleanliness! Use sterile growing medium. Remove and destroy affected plants, not just foliage. Kill with biological Serenade® and the Bordeaux mixture (copper sulfate and hydrated lime) is also somewhat effective.

Root Rot

Root rot turns roots dark brown, slows growth, leaves discolor, older foliage and later the entire plant wilts. Root rot is caused by lack of oxygen and soggy substrate.

Prevent root rot by using fresh, sterile growing medium and keeping the garden clean. Keep calcium levels adequate and avoid excess nitrogen. Keep pH above 6.0 in hydroponic units, and use Bio-Fungus® or RootShield®.

Spraying

Pests and diseases can often be avoided by making sure the garden area is clean. Inspect foliage and roots regularly for signs of pests and diseases. Control the growing environment to ensure plants are strong and healthy. Sometimes even with the best intentions, pests and diseases get a grip in the garden and must be removed.

Once you have determined you must spray, assess the damage and identify the pest or disease. Once identified, you can take cultural measures or purchase the proper product to rid the garden of the plague.

Root rot causes roots to turn brown and slimy.

- Use only contact sprays approved for edible fruits and vegetables
- DO NOT USE toxic systemic chemicals!
- Read the entire label on all sprays and follow directions
- Mix pesticides and fungicides just before using
- Safely dispose of unused spray
- Organic and natural-based sprays are also toxic and should be used sparingly
- Spray both sides of leaves and stems
- Rinse leaves on both sides with plain water 24 to 48 hours after spraying
- Use protective gear, including a facemask, when spraying, especially if using an aerosol/fogger
- Raise lamps up and out of the way

Small pump hand sprayers are convenient and economical.

Index

218

Acknowledgments

I would like to thank the growers not listed below who opened their garden doors to become part of this instructional guidebook. They provided ideas, photo opportunities, photos, knowledge, and some of the best buds in the world. Thank you, wonderful growers, from me and everyone who reads this book!

**Contributors, photographers and credits
are listed in alphabetical order:**

Aaron, Alan Dronkers, Alibaba, Aqualab, Arjan, Avalon W., Balta, Barbas, Barge, Barney's, Barry, Bean, Ben Dronkers, Betsy, Bill, BioGreen, Bob, BOG, Boy, Breeder Steve, Buddy, Bulldog Oakland, Canna, Cannabis College, Cañamo, Carlos, Charles, Charlie, Chicago, Chimera, Chris T., Chris V., Cliff, Conrad Hydroponics, D.J. Short, Damkring, Dany Danko, Darryll, David, Delicatessen Seeds, Dennis, Derry, Dick, DNA Genetics, Don C., Dutch Passion, Eddy Lepp, Elmar, Emilio, English – Canada BC, Estella, Eye Catching, Fabio, Felix, Ferran, Fran, Franco, Frank, Fred, Frenchie, GAP, Gaspar, Gato, Gerrit, GH, Gladys, Gregorio (Goyo) Fernandez, Gypsy Nirvana, Harmon, Harry, Henk, HESI, HIGH TIMES, Hugo, Isaac, J., Jaime Prats, Jaime, Jan Sennema, Jane, Javi, Jay, Jeff Jones, Jeff Tek, Jeff, Jens, Jimmy Chicago, John, Joint Doctor, Jordi, Jorge Cervantes, Jorge, Jose, Juan, K., Kyle, La Mota, Larry, Lars, LED Guy, Linda, Lorna, Los Sevillanos, Luc, Magus Genetics, Mama Editions, Marco Renda, Mario, Martin P., Martin Trip, Martin, Mauk, Michael, Michka, Miguel, Mike, Mila, Moises, Monsenor Jose Maria, Mona, Moño, Next Generation Seed Co., Nirvana Seeds, Oakland Buyer's Coop, Olaf, Ortue, Oscar, Osona Canem, Paradise Seeds, Patty C., Paul C., Peter, PHEC, Pollinator Company, R. Lee, Red, Reeferman, Rob Clarke, Roger Watanabe, Ron, Sam, Sebastian, Sensi Seeds, Sergio, Serious Seeds, Sesqueix Grow Shop, Shantibaba, Siglinde, Simon, Sirin, Skip, Soft Secrets, Soma, Stacey, Susan, Suzanne, THCene, The Greenhouse, THSeeds, Tigrame, Toni, Treating Yourself, Trichome Technologies, Vansterdan, Varnero, William, www.ledgrow.com, Xus, Z.

Who is Jorge Cervantes?

Jorge Cervantes developed his life-long fascination with cannabis as a university student in Mexico. After graduation, he moved to California in the 1970s where he became a "guerilla grower" of "sinsemilla" (Spanish for without seeds) marijuana, the "new" high-quality cannabis that Mexicans reserved for domestic consumption. In the early 1980s Cervantes started growing indoors with high intensity discharge (HID) lights to escape detection and control the environment, harvesting four crops the first year. A lack of credence and information about indoor cultivation led him to author *Indoor Marijuana Horticulture* in 1983.

Here are just a few of the milestones that mark his public career in the cannabis world during the last 25 years.

 1983 *Indoor Marijuana Horticulture* is published. The 96-page book, an instant best-seller, was dubbed "Indoor Grower's Bible" by growers.

 1985 Started writing for *High Times* magazine.

 1984 Jorge starts writing for *Sinsemilla Tips*

 1986 Jorge collaborates with Neville at the Cannabis Castle in Holland to launch the first color Seed Bank catalog published in 1987.

 **1985** Second edition of *Indoor Marijuana Horticulture* is published. Expanded to 224 pages.

 1986 Jorge persuades Neville, founder of the Dutch company The Seed Bank, to meet Steve Hagar; the next year Hagar founded the Cannabis Cup celebrated in Amsterdam, Holland.

 **1987** Jorge introduces horizontal reflective hoods in North America and cannabis growing gets 40% more light!

 1996 Jorge returns to Australia and sets up an underground distribution network for *Indoor Marijuana Horticulture.*

 1988 *Marihuana Binnen,* Dutch edition of *Indoor Marijuana Horticulture* is published.

 **1997** Started the website www.marijuanagrowing.com.

 1989 DEA "Operation Green Merchant" shuts down Jorge Cervantes' grow store and more than 40 other hydroponic stores in the USA.

 1998 Jorge moves to Canada to research and write. He starts writing for *Cannabis Culture* (formerly *Cannabis Canada*).

 **1990–1992** Jorge goes underground to research cannabis. He travels extensively throughout Europe, Latin America, North America, and Australia.

 1998 First edition of *Marijuana Indoors: Five Easy Gardens* is published.

 **1993** Third edition of *Indoor Marijuana Horticulture* is released. Jorge collaborates with Rob Clarke and Ed Rosenthal.

 1998 First articles appear in *Cañamo,* Spanish language marijuana magazine.

 1994 First edition of *Marihuana Drinnen & Draußen,* German edition of *Indoor Marijuana Horticulture* is published.

1999 Jorge reports on huge indoor grow operations and acres of marijuana growing outdoors in Switzerland and dispels the myth that Swiss grow bad dope!

1999 *Indoor Marijuana Horticulture* is the first cannabis grow book banned in Australia.

2000 First "Jorge's Rx" question and answer column published in *High Times* magazine. Jorge continues to write the column and feature articles for *High Times*.

2000 First edition of *Marijuana Outdoors: Guerrilla Growing* is published.

2001 First edition of *Marihuana en Exterior Cultivo de Guerrilla* Spanish edition of *Marijuana Outdoors: Guerrilla Growing* is published.

2001 Jorge contributes a large cannabis cultivation chapter to the French language book *Pourquoi & comment cultiver du chanvre.*

2002 First *Marihuana Cultivo en interior* Spanish edition of *Indoor Marijuana Horticulture* is published.

2002 Fourth edition of *Indoor Marijuana Horticulture* is published. Expanded to 384 pages and 200 color photos.

2003 Jorge starts European cannabis fair lecture circuit including: CannaTrade (Switzerland), Feria High Life Barcelona and Spannabis (Spain), Cannabis Cup and High Life (Holland), Interhanf (Germany), and Hemp Fair London (UK).

2003 First edition of *Marijuana Jorge's Rx* is published.

2003 United Kingdom edition of *Indoor Marijuana Horticulture* is published.

 2003 *Marihuana drinnen: Alles über den Anbau im Haus* (fourth edition of *Indoor Marijuana Horticulture*) is published in German.

 2004 *Indoor Marijuana Horticulture* is pirated by French Canadian company. Bogus bible distinguished by low quality photos and silver inside cover.

2005 First "Grow with Jorge Cervantes" regular column published in five editions of *Soft Secrets* magazine published in Dutch, English, French, Italian, and Spanish.

  2005 First articles published in many cannabis magazines worldwide: *Burst High* (Japan), *Cáñamo* and *Yerba* (Spain), *Cânhamo* (Portugal), *Heads* (Canada), *CC Newz, Redeye Express,* and *Weed World* (UK), *Grass Times, Grow!, Hanf,* and *Hanf Journal* (Germany), *High Life,* and *International Cannagraphic* (Holland).

2005 Jorge reports on high quality marijuana growing in Colombian jungle.

2005 *Culture en intérieur* by Jorge Cervantes is published in French.

2006 Jorge starts writing for Italian and English language *Dolce Vita* magazines.

2007 First *Marijuana: horticultura del cannabis La biblia del cultivador Médico de interior y exterior* Spanish edition of the fifth edition of *Marijuana Horticulture: the Indoor/Outdoor Medical Grower's Bible* is published.

2006 *Marijuana Horticulture: the Indoor/ Outdoor Medical Grower's Bible* is published. Expanded to 512 pages and 1,120 color images.

2006 *Jorge Cervantes' Ultimate Grow DVD* released. The 100-minute DVD shot in British Columbia, Canada set a new standard for DVD production.

2007 *Jorge Cervantes' Ultimate Grow DVD II* is released. The 100-minute DVD shot in Spain visits marijuana gardens only insiders can see.

2006 Jorge starts writing for *Oaksterdam News*.

2007 *Jorge Cervantes' Ultimate Grow DVD* is released in Russian.

2006 Jorge starts writing for German language *THCene* magazine.

2007 Jorge reports on high quality greenhouse growing operations in Mexico.

2007 *Culture en intérieur Basic Edition* by Jorge Cervantes is published in French.

 **2008** First *Jorge Cervantes' Cultivation Tips 2008 Ultimate Grow Calendar* published

 2007 *Culture en intérieur Master Edition* by Jorge Cervantes is published in French.

 2008 *Jorge Cervantes' Ultimate Grow DVD III* (3-box set) is released.

 2008 *Best of High Times Jorge Cervantes Grow Guide* is published.

 2009 Dutch *Marijuana Horticulture* is published

 **2008** First edition of *Marijuana: Orticoltura Indoor/Outdoor La Bibbia del coltivatore Medico,* Italian edition of *Marijuana Horticulture: The Indoor/Outdoor Medical Grower's Bible* is published.

 2009 Russian *Marijuana Horticulture* is published

 2009 First edition of *Marijuana Grow Basics: The Easy Guide for Cannabis Aficionados* is published in English

 **2008** Jorge celebrates 25 years (1983–2008) as a professional cannabis writer and photographer.

 2009 First edition of *Marijuana Grow Basics: The Easy Guide for Cannabis Aficionados* is published in German

 2010 *Marihuana Drinnen (Marijuana Horticulture)* available in German.

Outdoor Bonus Pages!

Seedlings and clones grown indoors are often moved outdoors. The following Outdoor Bonus Pages show some examples of growers that have moved their seedlings and clones outdoors.

Our Little Valley

This mountain guerrilla garden in British Colombia, Canada is just one of many!

Once hardened-off, indoor clones are moved to the outdoor guerrilla garden.

Amend the native soil with plenty of light soil.

After a summer of growth, plants are strong and flowering.

Moving supplies up to the garden is demanding dangerous work!

Beautiful purple hues dominate this Romulan x Timewarp bud.

Plants start to yellow during the last weeks of flowering.

Clandestine fields of cannabis dot the mountains in North America.

This big Romulan x Timewarp cross is close to harvest day.

Happy growers show the fruits of their labor.

Jack Herrer Screen of Green Plant

This single Jack Herrer clone is grown Screen of Green (ScROG) on a protected terrace. The clone was transplanted outdoors the first of June and harvested the seventh of October.

A super strong healthy clone is trellised to the sides of the container.

The plant continues to grow with a low profile towards the sides of the container.

In a week the seedling has grown beyond the edges of the container.

Now the plastic netting is added to continue to train this ScROG plant.

The healthy well-fed Jack Herer clone continues vegetative growth.

Days grow short and the first signs of flowering are seen as stems stretch.

Small buds start to form near the ends of branches.

Small buds are now visible.

The stem of this single plant has many branches and dense foliage.

Buds on branches are continuing to mature.

Foliage has overtaken the plastic screen once visible below.

Branches full of buds continue to develop in this rooftop garden.

Ten days from harvest and buds are filling out nicely.

Buds gain almost half their harvest weight during the last two weeks before harvest.

Here is a shot of the same Jack Herer seedling on harvest day!

Backyard Gardens
These back yard gardens are located in France and Spain.

This well-kept back yard garden has cannabis seedlings everywhere.

Planting next to a wall protects plants from wind and keeps them warmer at night.

Buds continue to mature in this country garden. The fence helps keep the garden private.

Haze cross shows sativa dominance.

Leaves yellow on this Green Ambassador bud that is a few days from harvest.

The buds on this Colombian sativa Shaman plant fill entire branches. Wind and a brick wall keep them warmer at night.

This beautiful Congolese plant is growing from a 5-gallon (20 liter) pot. The fence helps keep the garden private.

Skunk buds fill a vacant space behind a garage.

Giant Master Kush bud conceals the identity of the grower completely!

Swiss Marijuana Fields

For several years Swiss growers used a loophole in the law to grow hundreds of acres of marijuana outdoors. Today laws have changed and growers moved indoors.

Purple and green plants stand apart in this field of cannabis.

Plants wave in the sun as buds soak in potent Swiss alpine sunshine.

Tractors are essential when harvesting fields of cannabis!

This field in South Switzerland blends in with the countryside.

Three to five foot-tall (90-150 cm) plants are easier to maintain and harvest when growing on a large scale.

This ball of hash was collected from the manicurist's scissors.

The Swiss Alps rise virtually straight up on the other side of marijuana fields.

Bernard Rapaz (center) and Michka (left) are interviewed by German TV reporter in one of Rapaz' marijuana fields.

Ten-foot-tall (3 m) plants are dwarfed by Swiss Alps in the background.

Bud Photos and Patrons

Auto-flowering Feminized Taiga 2, Dutch Passion

Auto-flowering Feminized Tundra, Dutch Passion

Fresian, Dutch Passion

SnowBud, Dutch Passion

Support for legalization is **growing**.

Recent polls show over **43%**
of Americans support the
taxation and **regulation**
of marijuana.

Help sow the seeds of reform.
Join **NORML** today.

national organization for the
reform of marijuana laws
www.norml.org | 202.483.5500